European Community Design

European Community Design
*The Works of 12 European Community
Graphic Designers*

Edited by Wei Yew

© 1993

Published by Quon Editions © 1993

Printed in Singapore

Quon Editions
#203, 10107 – 115 Street
Edmonton, Alberta.
T5K 1T3 Canada.

ISBN 0-9694432-8-5

European Community Design
Includes bibliographical references and index.
ISBN 0-9694432-8-5
1. Design—Europe. 2. Designers—Europe. 3. Commercial art—Europe.
I. Yew, Wei, 1943-
NC998.6.E87E87 1992   741.6'092'24   C92-090334-7

European Community Design

The Works of

12 European Community

Graphic Designers

Edited by Wei Yew

Quon Editions

Design & Production *Studio 3 Graphics*

Contents

To Messrs. Arnodi, Bernard, Brattinga, Ferreira, Fiszman, Fletcher, Katzourakis, Lupi, Mendell, Narbona, O'Hanlon and Popov with sincere thanks.

Many thanks to:

Bonnie Bishop for editing the written word.

Mary Yeow-Forster for coordinating with all the designers and gathering the resources.

Preface

When Spain joined the European Community in 1992, a great economic union was established with no trade barriers between the member nations. With the increase in business activity comes an increase in demand for all services designers provide.

European Community Design features the leaders of graphic design in the European Community. It gathers the work of twelve very talented designers from their respective countries. Each designer's work is strong, individual and independent of current trends. All have a serious understanding of design and its philosophy, as the following excerpts reveal:

The dream is to participate in the commercial pollution with posters which clean up their surroundings. *Per Arnoldi*

We believe in the highest standards of quality ... It is by no means an easy task. In France today, graphic design is plagued with a plethora of commercial advertising in social and cultural sectors that exhibits the weak graphic design background of the decision makers.
Pierre Bernard

I view the artist, no matter what the medium, as someone who is always on the alert, signalling change and visually registering it in his or her own idiosyncratic fashion. *Pieter Brattinga*

... Oporto (where Ferreira was born) has developed a strong architecture and highly individual cultural tradition with its heritage of emancipation of the middle-class and the ideals of romanticism and liberalism. *Antero Ferreira*

A campaign for a product can be limited in time, whereas the brand identity demands permanence. The firm that adopts a 'fashionable' logo risks seeing its age prematurely. *Gilles Fiszman*

It's an intuitive process involving search, discovery, recognition, evaluation, and rejection of development. There are no specific rules or recipes; one might slip through a sequence of actions in seconds, or sweat through step by step. *Alan Fletcher*

New trends in the international market, the evolving focus of safety regulations and the ever shifting preferences of clients trying to keep abreast of fierce competitions, are the diverse sources ... to expand a creative talent.
Michael Katzourakis

I have found that the training of an architect often adds to my way of dealing with the work I do now – its three dimensional vision contributes to not accepting the imposition and limits of the typographical cage. *Italo Lupi (who went into graphic design shortly after graduating in architecture)*

Graphic design is not art, it is communication ... must be clear and unequivocal to be successful ... must get the message across ... must be understood by the general public.
Pierre Mendell

Technology is a crucial place for today's graphic designer to be. Icon-based graphical interfaces, screen design, on-line tutorials, hypermedia with sound and animation – these are logical extensions of the design arena. *Tony O'Hanlon*

I do not recognize any difference between my work as a designer and my work as a painter.
Josep Pla-Narbona

The idea for a poster comes mostly when I am walking in the street observing the people. I can link their reactions to an event, and later the idea comes to paper in graphic form.
Kamen Popov

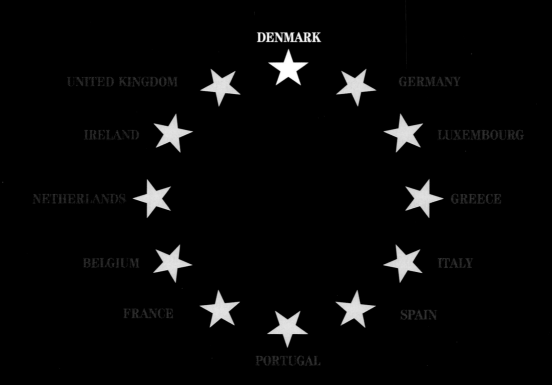

Per Arnoldi

Artist painter, graphic designer, TV host and raconteur, Per Arnoldi was born in Copenhagen in 1941. He is married to the Danish actress Christiane Rohde and they have one son who is a writer.

Arnoldi's poster work has been commissioned in New York by the Guggenheim Museum, Carnegie Hall, Lincoln Centre, and the American Jazz Orchestra, and in Japan for Jr. Hokkaido. Other poster designs range eclectically from the artistic associations of The American Ballet, The Royal Theatre of Copenhagen, The Chicago Symphony, to the business affiliations of Du Pont, Novo, Siemens, and DSB. Displays of Arnoldi's work are represented in the permanent collections of museums in nine countries including Britain, Germany, and the United States.

As a world-wide guest lecturer, Arnoldi's invitations have taken him to the Florida International University, University of Geneva, Tama University in Tokyo, the World Economic Forum in Davos, the Art Center in Montreux, the Bezalel Academy in Jerusalem, and the Chartered Designers Society in Hong Kong.

The short life of the poster could lead some to think it is also forgotten quickly. But fleeting arts have faithful lovers. The Bauhaus dream -to create things of quality, to shape all the elements of our surroundings with care -is not dead. The Nazis closed Bauhaus in 1937. Fifty years makes everything more clear/those whose past is murky hope for darkness/that which was clear still shines.

The poster makes use of visual and linguistic clichés. Clichés are collective pictures with a specific meaning for a specific group in a specific place at a specific time. Therefore, all available pictures are old ones, all words are known ones. The job is to combine. Minerva productions engaged me to design a poster announcing an educational film on AIDS. The ancient sign for love is the heart. I thought I could use it as a traffic sign: Caution, heart ahead. Then one could imagine a variation in traffic signs. "P" could stand for Parking, and an inverted "P" for No Parking. The heart for love and all that entails. The inverted heart for a warning. Something ahead, something dangerous. Watch out, pay attention. The neutrally geometrical heart deceived me. The traffic sign functioned, but also resembled a body part we hadn't intended to focus on. The sign can be inverted and turned against itself. The theory was better than the cliché.

The poster is here to stay...alive. Posters have a short life. Posters live close to their time. Pictures are time frozen. We did not know in the sixties, when the poster made its come-back as a powerful medium, that it was the sixties. It's not visible until it's visible. The poster's picture is not finished until something is missing. The text. A bad poster groans under a text which is in its way or excessive. A good poster cannot get enough. The dream is: To participate in the commercial pollution with posters which clean up their surroundings. That advertising can be expressed with a robust quality which can survive on the street, deliver a message, sell a product, and simultaneously send off a positive signal. Not change the world, participate in the good and the bad, but with decisions so clear, so aesthetically differently well-ordered that we can live with them....

The poster has had a strange life in Denmark. Helge Refn, Aage Rasmussen, Ib Andersen and Hallman created tremendous works. The thirties and forties flourished. Terrified of the violent poster jungle along the highways of France, Belgium and America, we made a panicky puritanical decision in the fifties in the hope of protecting the landscape and cities from being overwhelmed with billboards. Poster places vanished and with the physical frames vanished the belief in the poster as a medium. Artists sat back, dazed, not understanding what had hit them. The advertising pillars were allowed to decay.... The situation reversed. In 1975, as a natural part of a comprehensive design program, the Danish State Railway launched a very visible, annual, massive poster campaign. The stations once again became natural frames for graphic communication. Pillars and walls and gables followed. The poster was back.

The poster is a genre of its own, with its own rules and masters. An enormous tradition, without which I couldn't survive -some brilliant artists whom I neither can nor want to avoid. For posters there are some basic steps which I haven't invented myself or even understood as yet, which I still practise, and which I will briefly dance through. A poster always says something. It's not just for decoration. Without circumlocution, as directly, as simply and effectively as possible. Its contents have to come from somewhere and go somewhere. From the storyteller to the beholder: a message; an announcement; a suggestion. Or a warning to be conveyed.

PER ARNOLDI 100 POSTERS
THE ISRAEL MUSEUM
PALEVSKY DESIGN PAVILLION
JERUSALEM SPRING 1990

*100 Posters, one man
show in Jerusalem*

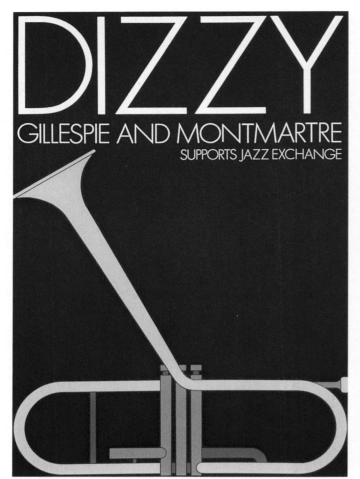

DIZZY
GILLESPIE AND MONTMARTRE
SUPPORTS JAZZ EXCHANGE

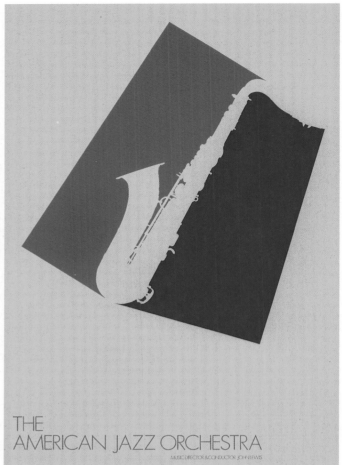

THE
AMERICAN JAZZ ORCHESTRA
MUSIC DIRECTOR & CONDUCTOR JOHN LEWIS

Posters

The Dizzy Gillespie poster was commissioned by Jazz Exchange, a small, boldly idealistic society that organised far-sighted, well-researched tours for European and American jazz musicians who were at the stage in their careers where both Europe and the USA were too far away for them to be booked as soloists.

The American Jazz Orchestra

Oscar Peterson's concert at the Montmartre Jazz Club

Listen Danish, Danish Composers Association, 1913-1988

OSCAR PETERSON
N.H.Ø.P.
PASS

SEPT.6.7.8.MONTMARTRE

LYT DANSK

1913 DANSK KOMPONIST FORENING 1988
KONCERTER I HELE LANDET · EFTERÅR 88 · MÅNEDSOVERSIGT FÅS PÅ BIBLIOTEKET

RANDERS BYORKESTER

JAZZ
MONTMARTRE COPENHAGEN

Posters

Randers City Orchestra

*Montmartre Jazz Club,
Copenhagen*

*Chicago Symphony
Orchestra Centennial*

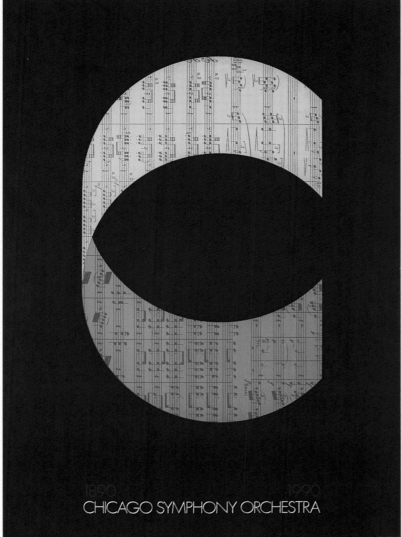

1890   1990
CHICAGO SYMPHONY ORCHESTRA

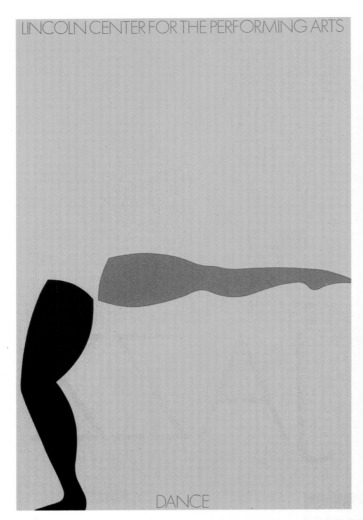

Posters

*Lincoln Center for the
Performing Arts: Dance*

*American Ballet Theatre,
50th birthday*

American Dance Festival

Poster

Hvidovre Theatre (design based on theatrical masks)

JR·HOKKAIDO + DSB·DENMARK

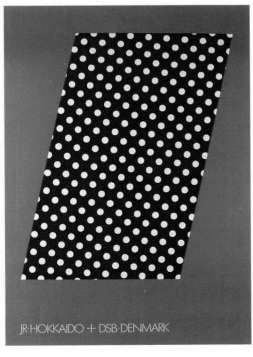

*JR Hokkaido + DSB,
a series of posters
commemorating the
affiliation between
Danish State Railways
and the Hokkaido Rail
Company*

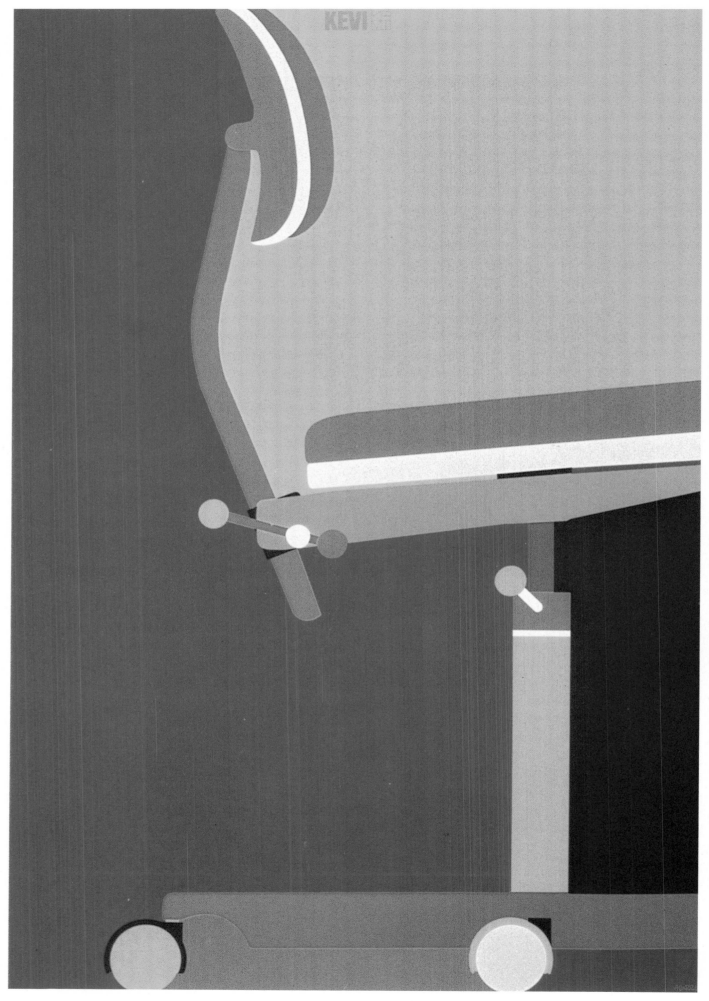

Poster   *The Kevi office chair*

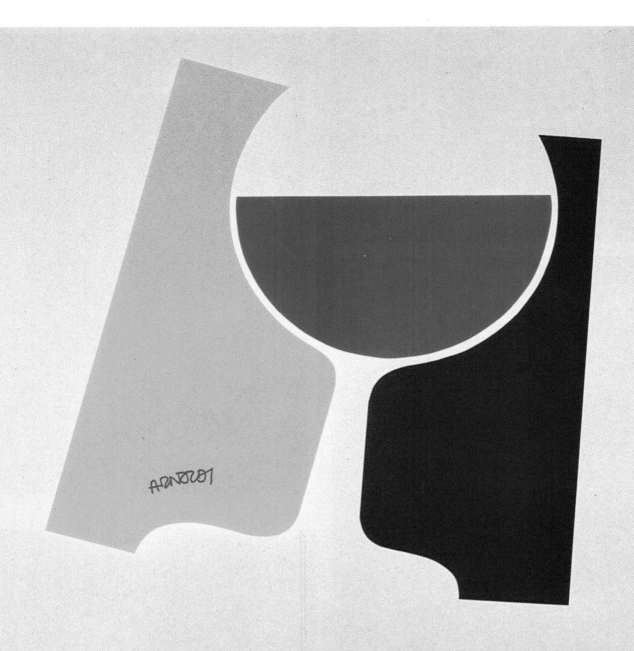

CHATEAU
ANDRON BLANQUET 1975
importé par
DET FRANSKE VINLAGER A/S

Poster

Det Franske Vinlager
(French wine)

*U.N. International World
Theatre Day, March 27,
1991*

Posters

*30 Years of Amnesty
International*

Aids Don't Catch It

*Save The Alps
Client: Alp Action/
Geneva + Newsweek
International*

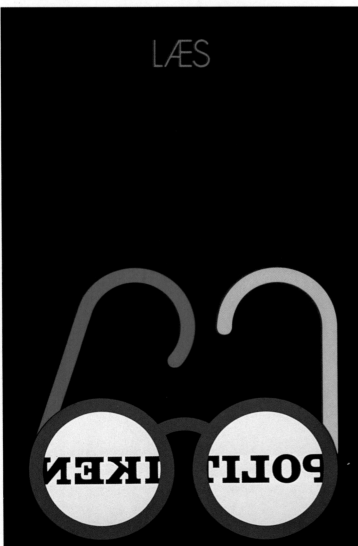

Posters

*Danish Furniture
Makers Quality Control
1959-1984*

*Copenhagen Don't Litter
Campaign*

*Læs Politiken (Read
Politiken), a
Copenhagen newspaper.
The publication's title
appears backwards
across the lenses of a
pair of eyeglasses,
suggesting that reading
the newspaper will
straighten out and
clarify the reader's
awareness of political
events.*

Steel Sculpture

Gajol licorice,
Copenhagen

Sculpture (painted
wood) for Rhone-Poulenc

Chair (folded steel)

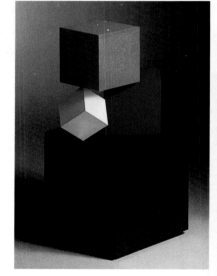

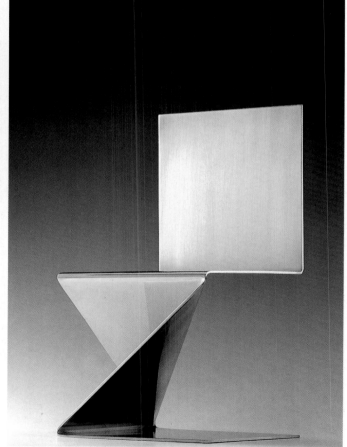

Newsweek cover for special issue, SWITZERLAND 700 YEARS

Packaging for Navigator software for IBM

DENMARK

GERMANY

LUXEMBOURG

GREECE

ITALY

FRANCE

SPAIN

PORTUGAL

Pierre Bernard

Pierre Bernard was born in Paris in 1942. He first studied at the Ecole Supérieure des Arts Décoratifs then continued his education in poster art at the Warsaw Academy in Poland with Henryk Tomaszewski. After receiving his Master's Degree from the Institute of Environment in Paris, Bernard formed the collective Grapus in 1970. Grapus has been the recipient of numerous awards and prizes including: Warsaw Biennale, Brno Biennale, Colorado Biennale, Lahti Biennale, Zagreb Zgraf, NY ADC, and Toyama Triennale. In 1991 Grapus transformed itself into three different groups of which the Atelier de Création Graphique is a distinctive branch of the collective.

From left to right: Fokke Draaijer, Agnes Korink, Julie de La Celle, Sylvain Enguehard, Dominique Soubranne, Pierre Bernard, Virginie Jaïs, Anne Drucy, Dirk Behage. Photographer: Michel Chassat

Upon his return from Europe in 1929, Eleazer Markovitch Lissitzky said to an assembly of architects in Moscow, "At that time, the sentiment and consciousness of our new generation of architects bore the stamp of the cultural revolution's vast experiments. An artist's work has no value, finality or beauty in and by itself. Its whole worth comes strictly from the bonds it weaves with the community. The architect's hand is visible in any great work, but that of the community is implicit. What artists and creators invent never comes down to them from heaven. And this is why we understand 'reconstruction' to mean control over what is unclear, 'mysterious', and chaotic both in our architecture and in our lives. Our goal is to create a social order, that is, to bring to consciousness that which belongs to the realm of instinct."

I have made this theory my belief. The successive graphic expressions that history has brought forth represent the moments in which there is a sociological and historical change in society. Expressions of those moments are the fruits. It is the duty of graphic designers and architects to act upon their times. In January of 1991, I founded with Dirk Behage and Fokke Draaijer, the Atelier de Création Graphique which we continue to run in the tradition of a creative collective. All our work is signed: Atelier de Création Graphique-Grapus.

We believe in the concept of public information based on a respect for the highest standards of quality. We always hope to find our clients among those whose vocation or ethical sense it is to adhere to this type of approach to communication. It is by no means an easy task. In France today, graphic design is plagued with a plethora of commercial advertising in social and cultural sectors that exhibits the weak graphic design background of the decision makers. This plethora and ignorance are for the sole financial benefit of the advertisers and lead to a growing confusion among our potential clients who are increasingly surrounded by kitsch and ephemeral signs. In the midst of such chaos, Atelier de Création Graphique makes high claims, "We are interested in all those areas of graphic design which convey a type of communication centering on a questioning of social value."

Given that graphic designers must, by definition, be involved in contemporary society, we believe it is necessary to develop both creative attitudes and to try and combine them harmoniously, not only to find answers to concrete problems, but also to throw light on the future.

Graphic design implies a sequence of activities in which various steps interact with each other and determine the qualitative result. A creative studio needs a creative client, a creative printer...and a creative public. In this respect, as well, what is obvious to us actually bucks the general trend when profit is the primary concern, and few are those who share our view of the profession. Fortunately those who do, be it clients or suppliers, can very quickly turn into allies. On a given project their requirements complement ours and vice versa. All conditions are met for a wonderful experience to be attempted and carried through to a successful completion. A shared concern for quality fosters a very enjoyable relationship between the one who places the order, the graphic designer, and the manufacturer. The product is cumulative proof of the respect each has for the public.

The key to success lies, in my opinion, in this principle of positive commitment to the public. Such a commitment is essential if a social contract is to turn into a cultural act, which can only be generous and therefore hazardous.

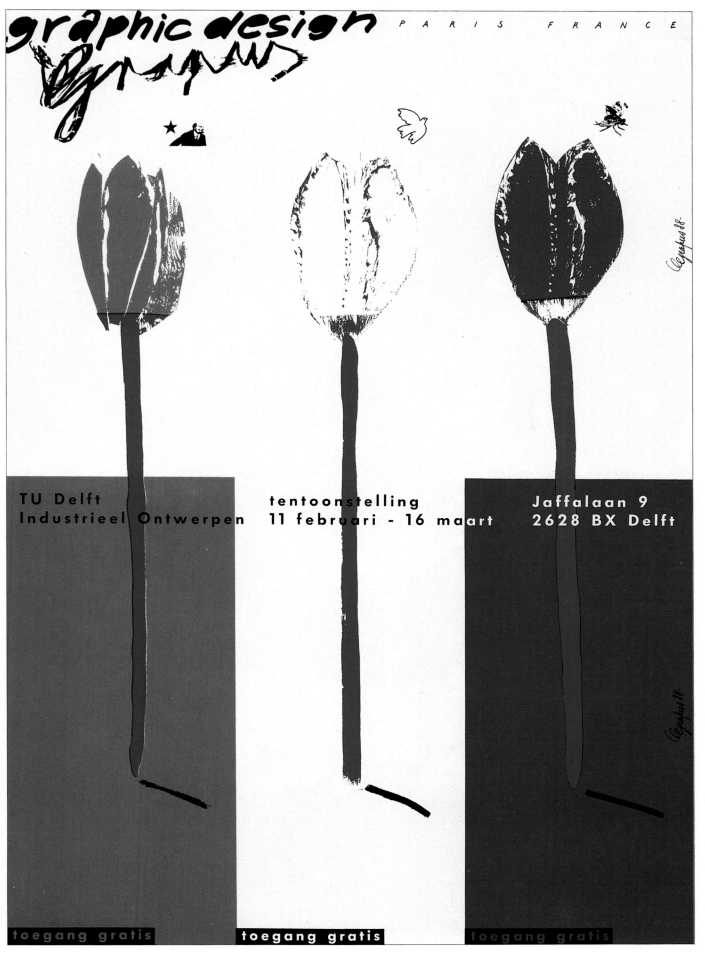

Poster

*Announcement of a
Grapus exhibition in
Delft, Holland*

General emblem of Parcs
Nationaux de France

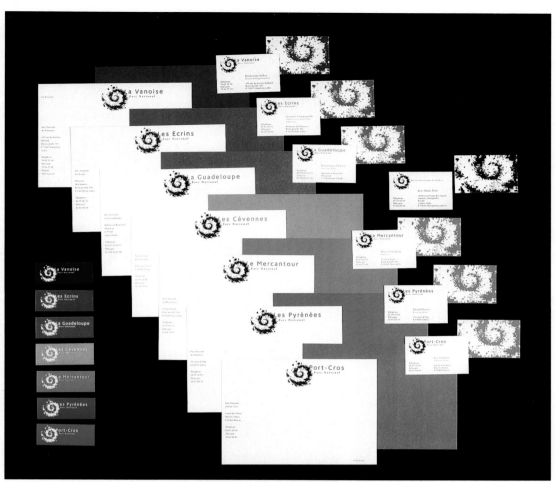

Correspondence cards
and business cards

Police badge for the park-
rangers

Parcs Nationaux de
France: an emblem, an
identity

Sign system

Parcs Nationaux de
France – General
problematic overview

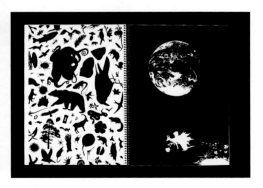

Louvre Museum

Souvenir Guide for the collections from the seven departments

Letterheads for Administration and Departments

Presentation brochure for the Museum's new policy

Poster
The Louvre Donors

Poster
"Prepare your visit with us"

Orientation guides in 6 different languages

Banner outside the museum

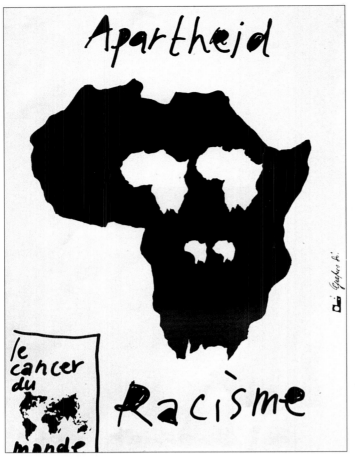

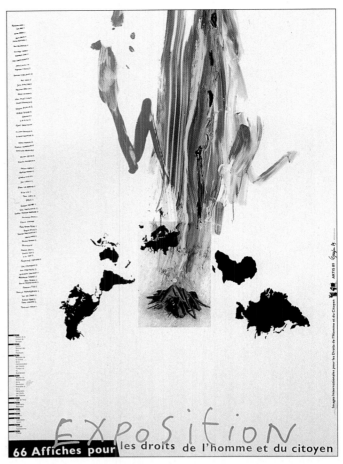

Posters

Apartheid – Racism

*Exhibition – 66 posters
for human and citizen
rights*

*Grapus Show –
Group exhibition at the
Poster Museum of Paris*

Glanzend

Paper Cream

'Parilux'

JOB - Parilux

Premium art coated French paper

Gloss card leaflet

Ivory card leaflet

2-tone card leaflet

Couché véritable **Two Tone**

Couché véritable **Two Tone**

Annual International
Graphic Design Festival
of Chaumont. The
festival has been in
existence for four years.

Letterheads of the 1991
Festival

Movie poster

Letterheads of the 1990
Festival

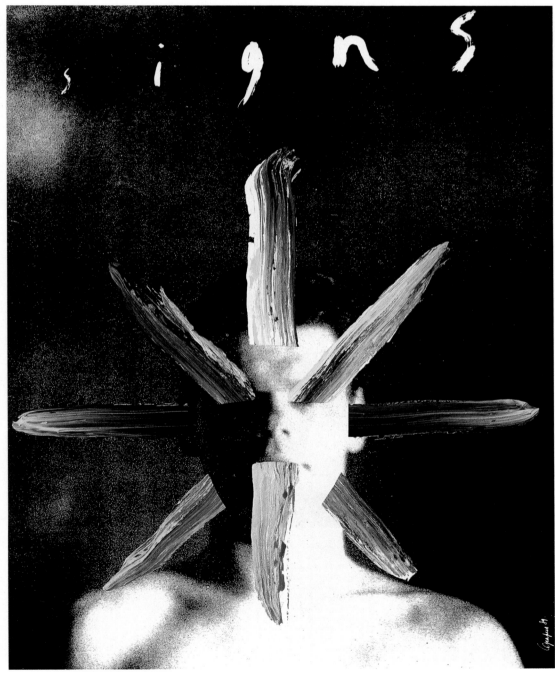

Graphic Design World Views – Cover for the ICOGRADA's anniversary book

Front cover of the TOTAL magazine about signs

Front and back covers of Japanese magazine "Tategumi Yokogumi" (Horizontal Vertical)

Book cover for "Terre étrangère", a collection of foreign literature translated into French

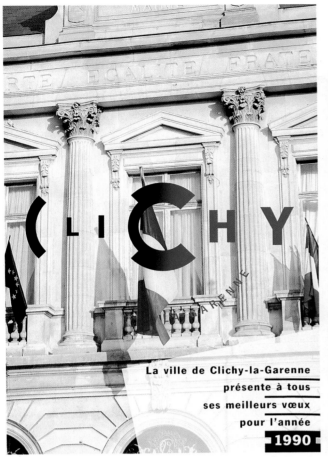

La ville de Clichy-la-Garenne présente à tous ses meilleurs vœux pour l'année **1990**

Numéro 1 janvier 1990 • Prix : 15 F

CLICHY

Magazine

Graphic identity for Clichy-la-Garenne, a city in the close suburb of Paris

Greetings from the city

City monthly magazine cover

Gift watch

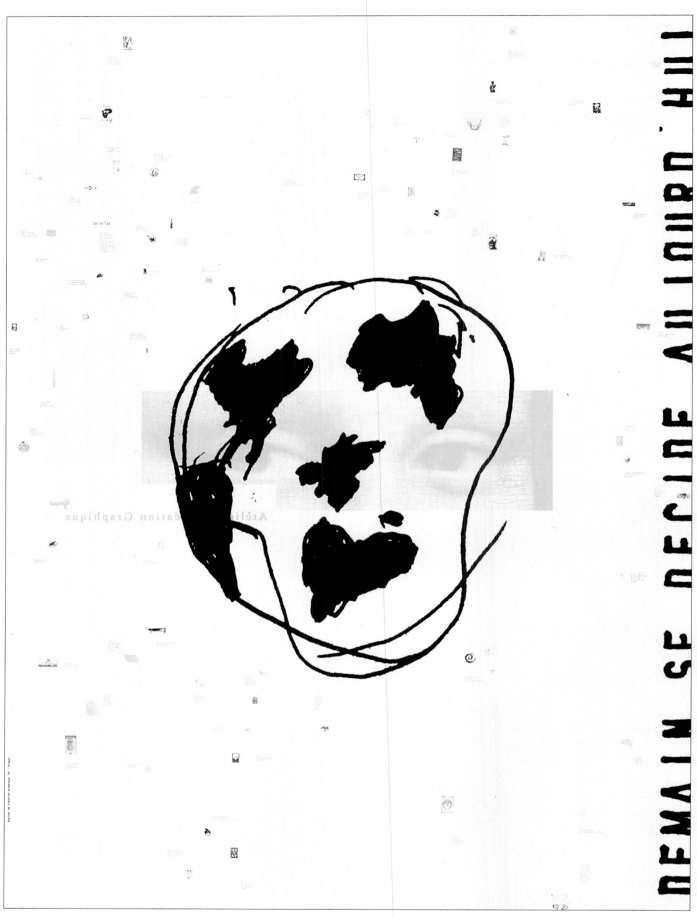

Poster

Tomorrow is decided today. Exhibition

Double-sided poster presenting the work of Atelier de Création Graphique - Grapus.

Placed side by side, the front and back of the poster form a 240 x 160cm poster. Typography connects both sides.

EXPOSITION de l'Atelier de Création Graphique '91 - Grapus
à l'Institut d'Art Visuel - Orléans - du 16 avril au 10 mai '91
(16) 38 53 49 07

Atelier de Création Graphique

DENMARK

UNITED KINGDOM

GERMANY

IRELAND

LUXEMBOURG

NETHERLANDS

GREECE

BELGIUM

ITALY

FRANCE

SPAIN

PORTUGAL

Pieter Brattinga

Pieter Brattinga was born in 1931 in Hilversum. In 1939 his father became the owner of Steendrukkerij de Jong & Co., a medium-sized printing company. As the owner's son, Brattinga quickly grew familiar with the day-to-day running of the company, printing techniques, and became acquainted with visiting clients and artists. After finishing his formal studies, Brattinga travelled to London where he studied drawing, painting and art history. In Paris at George Lang Printers, and at Fotolithografische Inrichting Koningsveld in Lieden, he learned the practical ropes of the printing trade. In 1951 he returned to work at de Jong & Co., and in the years to follow set on a course of international recognition.

Brattinga has been elected to sit on many national and international boards. His membership includes the Dutch Graphic Designers Association, de Alliance Graphique Internationale, the Art Directors Club Nederland, of which he was co-founder, and the Art Directors Club in New York. In 1960 Brattinga accepted an invitation to lecture on typography at Pratt University in New York. During his four years in the U.S., he also worked as correspondent for De Artistieke Staalkaart, an arts programme for the socialist VARA broadcasting network. Appointed many honours, Brattinga was chairman of a discussion panel on design training at the first congress of the International Council of Graphic Design Associations (ICOGRADA) in Zurich. In 1966 he was nominated the council's secretary-general and held that position for four years, and was part of the jury for the 1970 Warsaw Biennale.

In the late sixties, Brattinga founded the company Form Mediation International, subtitled Management Consultants for Art and Design. Over the years Form Mediation has carried out many varied commissions. Though Brattinga regularly designs posters, books, brochures, house-styles, and postage stamps he also organises exhibitions, collaborates on unusual publications about art and culture, is active in art education, runs a gallery for experimental printing, manages the copyright of a famous writer of children's books, writes books and articles for journals and festschrifts.

Brattinga's
philosophy: creativity. His aim is to stimulate
other people's creativity using simple means.
He gives people the instructions to do it
themselves. In all his activities, Brattinga puts
the emphasis on the experimental, which
appeals to the imagination of the other person,
and awakens the creative abilities which are
there in rudimentary form. Brattinga is a
'creative organizer' who has given himself the
social task of making the lives of his fellowmen
more pleasant by spurring them on to self-
activity. Pieter Brattinga wants to exchange
ideas in a functional manner, to put them
across and bring about communication. His
ability to communicate information graphically
serves him well in this aspect. The recipient is
always allowed to interpret for himself because
Brattinga doesn't permit his own ideas to
interfere with the message.

He is active in various fields and will not
restrict himself to one discipline. This diversity
gives Brattinga a distinct position in the Dutch
art world. Over the years he has built up a
reputation with eclectic projects in the field of
art, graphic and industrial design. The
journalist Jan Vrijman once wrote of
Brattinga's way of working that, "...his
functionality keeps him from confusion and
lack of control, his creative credo precludes
sterility." Brattinga views the artist, no matter
what the medium, as someone who is always
on the alert, signalling change and visually
registering it in his or her own idiosyncratic
fashion. He has never concerned himself much
with the artists who withdraw themselves to
ivory towers, and simply express their own
mental anguish. Rather, he admires those who
are on the frontline, eager to experiment and
take up challenges -those who have the
courage of their convictions to reject
preconceived ideas of art in order to make a
clear statement on the elusive changing world
for the benefit of their fellow men. His views

are similar to the Bauhaus credo: "Kunst und
Technik eine neue Einheit" -Only the artist
who makes use of new technology can
participate constructively in helping to create
a new world.

Brattinga has fears, though, of the new
technology that has created over-
specialisation. Large scaled production and
scientific management sweep aside smaller
working units hence, a plethora of specialists
working in isolation and responsible only for a
small part of the whole. During interviews, or
when lecturing, he often tells the story of two
Americans, one a famous atomic scientist, the
other an accountant, living next to one
another. Apart from passing the time of day
have nothing to say to each other. Brattinga is
convinced that over-specialisation creates a
narrowing of awareness and can greatly
endanger the process of interaction between
people. These social developments continue to
motivate Brattinga to act as an intermediary
for individuals and groups wishing to
communicate in the field of art and culture.

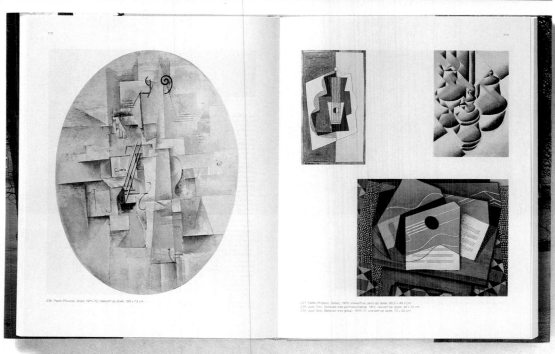

Book

*Kröller-Müller, hundred
years of building and
collection*
*Client: Joh. Enschedé &
Zonen, Haarlem*

Book

A documentary on Sandberg who has meant so much to Dutch art and culture. Brattinga was given a prestigious award for the design of this book by the Internationale Buchkunst Ausstellung in Leipzig where each year the 50 best produced books in the world are exhibited.

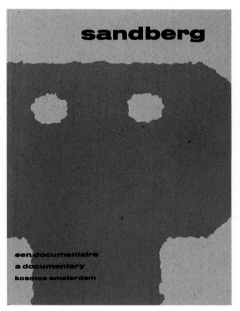

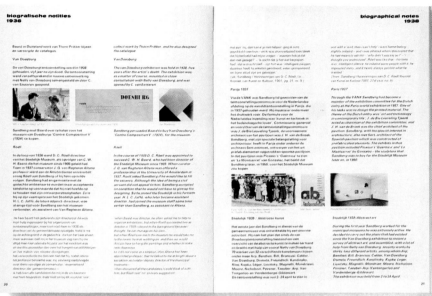

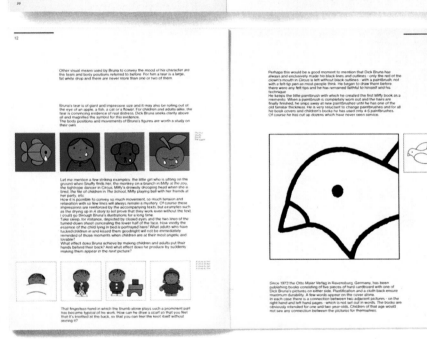

Children's books by Dick Bruna
Client: Mercis Ltd.

Postage stamps – PTT,
the Netherlands

*Statute for the Kingdom
of the Netherlands*

*Commemorating the
60th birthday of Prince
Bernhard*

*Commemorating Queen
Juliana's silver jubilee
as head of state*

*Jubilee Post Savings
Bank*

*Commemorating the
40th anniversary of
liberation of the
Netherlands*

*Commemorating the
50th wedding
anniversary of Princess
Juliana and Prince
Bernhard*

Netherlands

Pieter Brattinga

Christo : Surrounded Islands

Biscayne Bay, Greater Miami, Florida 1980 - 1983. Foto's van Wolfgang Volz. Een documentaire tentoonstelling.

Rijksmuseum Kröller-Müller Otterlo. 18 augustus tot 29 september 1985

foto: Wolfgang Volz. ontwerp: Pieter Brattinga. druk: steendrukkerij de Jong & Co., Hilversum 1985

Exhibition poster for the Rijkmuseum Kröller-Müller, Otterlo

Honderd tekeningen uit het Museum of Modern Art, New York

Rijksmuseum Kröller-Müller, Otterlo
van 15 april tot 18 juni 1973

Wessel Couzijn

Rijksmuseum Kröller-Müller, Otterlo, 27 sept. tot 16 nov. 1986

Posters

Exhibition poster for the Rijkmuseum Kröller-Müller, Otterlo: Hundred drawings from the Museum of Modern Art, New York

Exhibition poster for the Rijkmuseum Kröller-Müller, Otterlo

Exhibition poster for the Rijkmuseum Kröller-Müller, Otterlo

Claes Oldenburg: **Mouse Museum/Ray Gun Wing**

Rijksmuseum Kröller-Müller, Otterlo

17 juni tot 30 juli 1979

Bruce Nauman, 1972-1981

Rijksmuseum Kröller-Müller, Otterlo
van 5 April tot 25 Mei 1981

Posters

*Exhibition poster for the
Rijkmuseum Kröller-
Müller, Otterlo*

*Exhibition poster for the
Rijkmuseum Kröller-
Müller, Otterlo*

*Exhibition poster for the
Rijkmuseum Kröller-
Müller, Otterlo:
Sculpture 1948-1988
Carel Visser*

De Stijl 1917-1931
Rijksmuseum Kröller-Müller, Otterlo

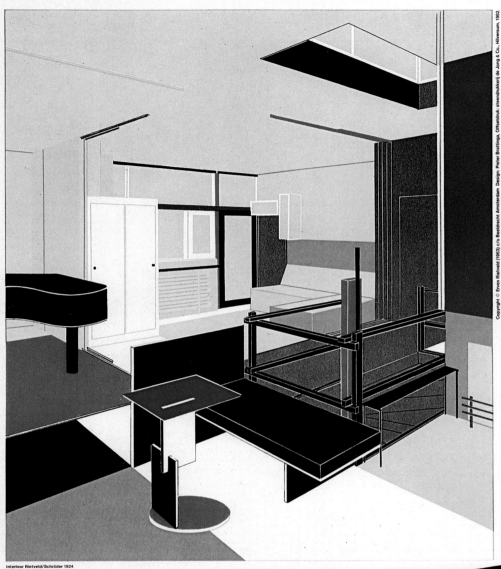

Interieur Rietveld/Schröder 1924

8 augustus tot 4 oktober 1982

De 1917-1923 periode in het Stedelijk Museum te Amsterdam
Periode 1923-1931 in het Rijksmuseum Kröller-Müller, Otterlo

Copyright © Erven Rietveld (1963) c/o Beeldrecht Amsterdam Design: Pieter Brattinga, Offsetdruk: steendrukkerij de Jong & Co., Hilversum, 1982.

Poster

*Exhibition poster for De
Stijl at the Rijkmuseum
Kröller-Müller, Otterlo*

*Exhibition: Sculpture
from Africa and Oceania*

Detail of the façade of Print Gallery, Pieter Brattinga, Amsterdam

Print Gallery – Information cube, closed.

Print Gallery – Information cube, opened.

Horizontally hinged door in preparation for lunch in the gallery

Brattinga's office on the first floor of the gallery

Antero Ferreira

Antero Ferreira was born in Oporto, Portugal in 1963. He graduated in Communication Design/ Graphic Arts from the Oporto Fine Arts School where he lectures in Design. In 1991 he was honoured as Visiting Designer at the Nova Scotia College of Art and Design in Canada. Ferreira is member of several artistic and professional associations such as APD (Portuguese Designer Association), AIGA (American Institute of Graphic Arts), New York, and The Next Generation of Icograda, Amsterdam.

Between 1986 and 1989 he received seven national awards and in 1989, mounted an exhibition of his work at the Museum of the Oporto Fine Arts School. Since that time he has taken part in several international exhibitions and is currently preparing for another individual showing in Oporto.

Antero Ferreira belongs to a new generation of Portuguese graphic designers which, in the last few years, have become known for their individual creations. Oporto, where Ferreira was born and continues to make his home, is the economic and social centre of a heavily industrialized region, where some of the most important financial projects are set. Ferreira's training and professional life have taken place in this cultural and aesthetic atmosphere, with its essential elements of urban growth. Oporto has developed a strong architecture and highly individual cultural tradition, with its heritage of emancipation of the middle-class and the ideals of romanticism and liberalism. The result has been an enlarged communication paradigm which demands of its designers a versatility which Ferreira thrives on and excels at.

As a student in the late eighties, the works Ferreira produced included illustration, posters, and development of graphic images. There is a preference for eclecticism, together with plasticity and analysis of reality, all of which are qualities of reflection. Into the nineties his works became more systemized and organized themselves around areas such as corporate identity, catalogues, brochures, posters, and publicity. The more frequent use of photography and information characterizes the designer's current work, whose expansion and success have led to the creation of an individual studio with the signature ANTERO FERREIRA DESIGN. Management criteria of Ferreira's career as a graphic designer are two-fold: within each project he considers different techniques and concepts and does a study of each work which takes into account the various formal and aesthetic implications of the end product; and he has developed a strategy of establishing relationships with international associations and institutions which evaluate and legitimize graphic arts.

The work he has produced in the past two years shows adaptability which is an essential feature of this artist. The graphic works use predominantly dark geometrical and sometimes very sober elements, other works base themselves on movement of the line. His intense collaboration with the photographer Oscar Almeida stands as a symbol for his preference for team work and centres on an interpretative and analytical approach. As Ferreira goes from concept to matter, from fragility to the objectivity of the line, from disorder to structured images, he reveals his maturity as an artist. And it is ultimately from this growth that the obvious high quality of his work is derived.

FANTASPORTO '89 IX FESTIVAL INTERNACIONAL DE CINEMA DO PORTO

3/12 FEVEREIRO · AUDITÓRIO NACIONAL CARLOS ALBERTO E CINEMAS LUMIÉRE

Organização CINEMA NOVO. Alto Patrocínio CÂMARA MUNICIPAL DO PORTO, DIRECÇÃO GERAL DO TURISMO, INSTITUTO DE PROMOÇÃO TURÍSTICA, FUNDAÇÃO CALOUSTE GULBENKIAN, GOVERNO CIVIL DO PORTO, MINISTÉRIO DA JUVENTUDE, INSTITUTO DA JUVENTUDE E SECRETARIA DE ESTADO DA CULTURA, DELEGAÇÃO REGIONAL DO NORTE DA SEC E INSTITUTO PORTUGUÊS DE CINEMA

Poster

*International
Fantastique Film
Festival*

AUDIOVISUAL LISBOA 88
Festival de Cinema e Vídeo da Cidade de Lisboa

Forum Picoas 11 a 20 de Novembro de 1988
Organização da Federação Portuguesa de Cinema e Audiovisuais

Posters

*International Video and
Film Festival*

*Poster announcing a
party of the end of the year
Client: Haus Amnésia*

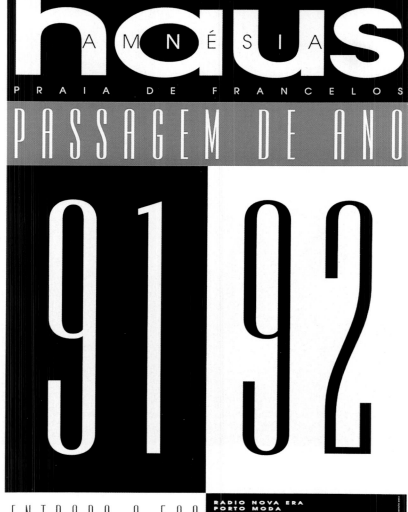

haus
AMNÉSIA
PRAIA DE FRANCELOS
PASSAGEM DE ANO
91 92
ENTRADA 2.500

RADIO NOVA ERA
PORTO MODA
QUANDO-QUANDO
P.O.A
GARRAFEIRA DO CAMPO ALEGRE
METROPOLITANA RADIOS

FANTASPORTO '88
VII FESTIVAL INTERNACIONAL DE CINEMA DO PORTO

12/21 FEVEREIRO 1988 · AUDITÓRIO NACIONAL CARLOS ALBERTO E CINEMA LUMIÉRE

Poster

*International
Fantastique Film
Festival*

Catalogue
Client: Soprenda

Mail order catalogue
Client: Donomo

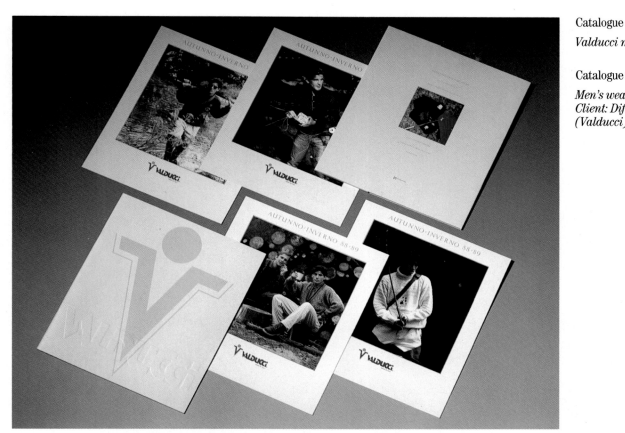

Catalogue
Valducci men's wear

Catalogue
Men's wear
Client: Difusõo Moda
(Valducci)

Catalogue

*For a fashion designer
Client: Difusõo Moda
(Valducci)*

Poster

*Fashion designer
collection (designers:
Antero Ferreira,
Constanza Puglisi)
Client: Nuno Gama*

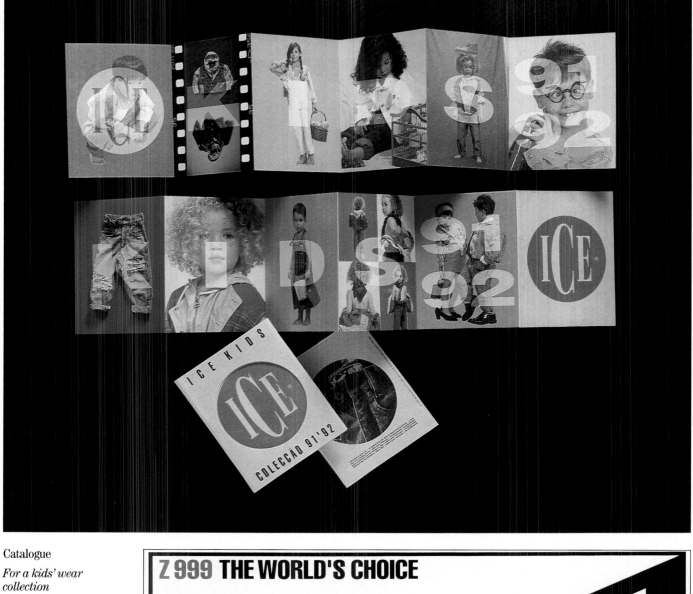

Catalogue

For a kids' wear collection
Client: Infesveste (ICE)

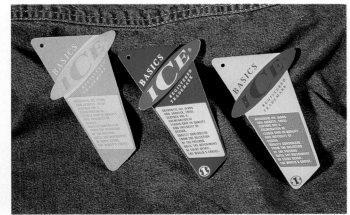

Labels

For jeans and jackets
Client: Infesveste (ICE)

Catalogue

For a design agency
Client: PSI

Poster

Company selling
revetment products

Poster

Surfing championship

DENMARK

UNITED KINGDOM

GERMANY

IRELAND

LUXEMBOURG

NETHERLANDS

GREECE

BELGIUM

ITALY

FRANCE

SPAIN

PORTUGAL

Gilles Fiszman

Gilles Fiszman was born in 1932 in Brussels. He studied in Warsaw, Poland, for five years at the Academy for Plastic Arts and was an interior decorator and display window specialist until 1960, when he returned to Brussels and took up the position of Creative Director for an advertising agency. Since that time he has made a celebrated name for himself working as a free-lance graphic consultant. He is partner of the AXION network, which has bases in Brussels, Montreal, Toronto, San Francisco, and New York, founder of Bureau Fiszman & Partners, and was a professor at ENSAV "La Cambre," where he taught the course 'Graphic approach to information'.

Fiszman served as president of Belgium's Graphists Union, and is a member of the Board of Managers Brussels Design Centre.

Psychological aspects and connotations do exist in our trade. You don't work on a flabby logo for a company which considers itself aggressive, nor a sharp image for a company that wishes to inspire confidence. It seems to me that this aspect of psychology is essential in as much as people receive and decode the image unconsciously, without analysing it as we designers do. From another point of view, you must bear in mind the motivation of the decision-maker or company head, who often (it's very human) chooses spontaneously according to his personality. You must make him understand that personal taste comes after company needs. A sphere expresses something different than a cube or a pyramid. The pyramid, for example, is the only geometrical volume that cannot be put out of shape. People don't realise this consciously perhaps. The pyramid resting on its base expresses more of a concept of stability while a sphere in space signifies lightness.

Advertising creates messages of relatively short life-span, while we creators of logos are working for the company and continuity. A campaign for a product can be limited in time, whereas the brand identity demands permanence. The firm that adopts a 'fashionable' logo risks seeing it age prematurely. In fact the first professional identities were emblems of the corporation which go back to the Middle Ages. But they only had one use, as an ensign. The Corporation gave an image of itself through their ensigns. Initially, the corporation was not an authority, but a grouping of interests. The fame of the corporation had to be established. Going back further, we can trace the first symbolic identities to the rallying-signs, like the shell of the pilgrims of St. James of Santiago de Compostela. This famous shell of St. James would, much later, become a symbol of the petroleum company Shell.

The creation of corporate identity demands a multi- or pluri-cultural understanding of the problems of communication. Cars, for example, are not sold the same way in the Northern countries as they are in South, East or West. A car is comfort, road holding, fuel consumption and a look. In other words a whole series of parameters that do not have the same value all over.

Once, I had to design the signs in a hospital for Beduins of the National Guard. After learning about the project, I went down there to fully understand the cultural factors, in particular the taboos that exist. While working with an Arab sociologist, we realised that bilingual English and Arabic signs would not be enough and that it was necessary to add a pictographic code because a considerable number of the Beduins were illiterate. The question of the signs was very important because the project was a one-storey building with several kilometres of corridors. For this labyrinth I incorporated a pebble language used in the desert by the Beduins. I used white pellets on a coloured background to represent the different departments of the hospital. Communication is a cultural act and consequently it must take the cultures in which it evolves into account if it is going to be effective.

Greeting Card

*Using folding
techniques, coloured
paper and combinative
graphics; the figure 6
changes into a 9 and
becomes the sun of the
year 69*

Institut d'Etudes de la Famille
et des Systèmes Humains, Bruxelles
Congrès International

Approches thérapeutiques
et modèles de formation
en thérapie familiale

22-24 septembre 1983/Bruxelles

Nathan Ackerman Institute
for Family Therapy, New York
International Conference

Therapeutic approaches
and training models
in family therapy

September 22-24 1983/ Brussels

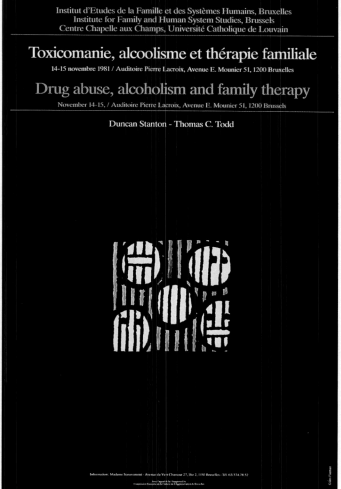

Institut d'Etudes de la Famille et des Systèmes Humains, Bruxelles
Institute for Family and Human System Studies, Brussels
Centre Chapelle aux Champs, Université Catholique de Louvain

Toxicomanie, alcoolisme et thérapie familiale

14-15 novembre 1981 / Auditoire Pierre Lacroix, Avenue E. Mounier 51, 1200 Bruxelles

Drug abuse, alcoholism and family therapy

November 14-15, / Auditoire Pierre Lacroix, Avenue E. Mounier 51, 1200 Brussels

Duncan Stanton - Thomas C. Todd

Institute for Family
Studies and Human
Systems

*The logo expresses the
double concept of an
open and interactive
system and illustrates
the systematic approach
of the institute. Posters
announcing congresses
and seminars aimed at
professionals in family
therapy, and
programme flyers.*

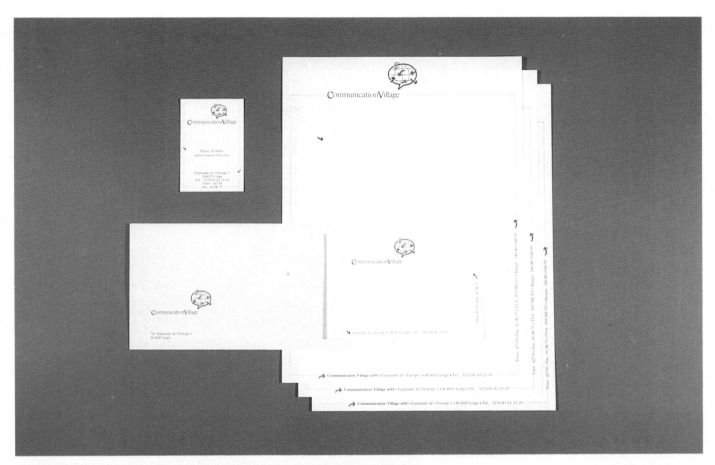

Communication Village Exhibition

The phylactery, containing the globe symbol around which a flood of multi-directional arrows are shooting, is an expression of universal communi-cation. Stationery, and T-shirt worn by mainly young personnel, making identification and recognition easy.

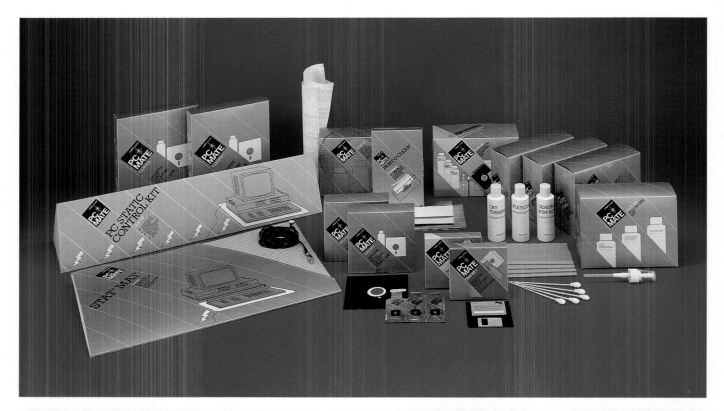

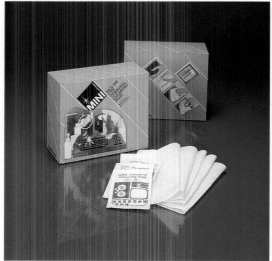

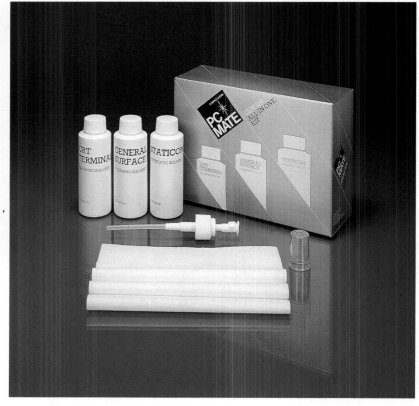

PC Mate computer
maintenance products

*For this range of
products aimed at
professionals, general
public and young people,
Bureau Fiszman &
Partners adopted a tone
which is both technical
and didactical, while
keeping a perfect visual
coherence. The diagonal
structure and the black
square motif are the
graphic constants of the
whole. The professional
products are presented
soberly on a metallised
colour background,
while the range of
products for the general
public is presented in a
loud, bright and
colourful way.*

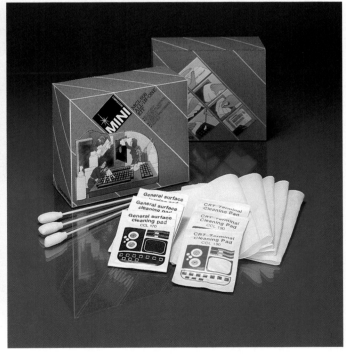

Belgian State's Gift Book

The Belgian State sees the need to establish its name. This prestigious gift book is offered to noted guests of the country and distributed in the Belgian diplomatic representations abroad. The book opens with chapters dealing with the history, political and economic organisations of the country. Each chapter is preceded by a little page illustrated with the portrait of a famous Belgian.

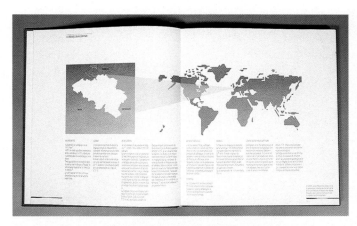

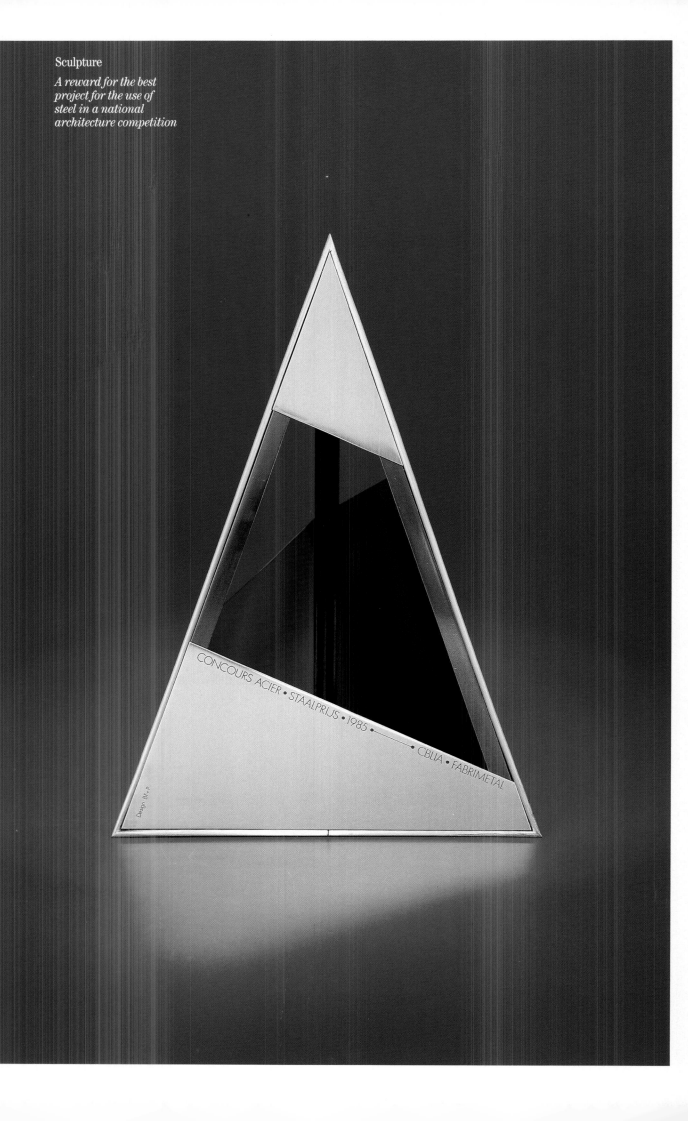

Sculpture

*A reward for the best
project for the use of
steel in a national
architecture competition*

CONCOURS ACIER • STAALPRIJS • 1985 • CBLIA • FABRIMETAL

Design BE+P

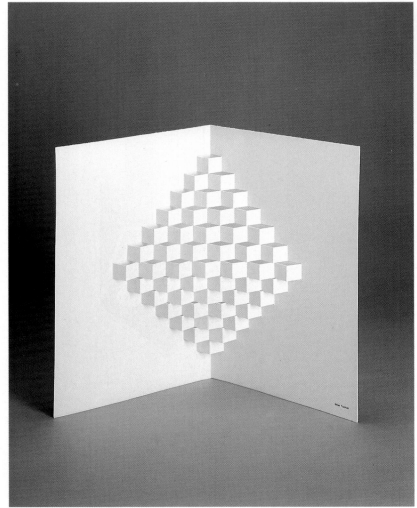

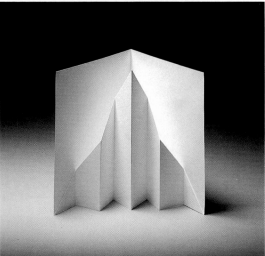

Greeting cards

LEVIS *(Belgian brand of paint)*

LEVIS identification on a shop-window and a close-up of the neon-sign

Creation of a signal system based on the symbol of the hand as the basic painting tool. The hands always indicate the direction of the front door of the shop.

SIGNALETIEK
De hand:
beschrijving, kleuren

Een signalisatiesysteem gebaseerd op het symbool van de hand articuleert zich rond het embleem. Dit systeem deklineert zich volgens zeven manieren die hiertegenover en op de volgende bladzijde afgebeeld zijn.
Deze elementen zullen zowel binnen als buiten de verkooppunten gebruikt worden. De dikte van de vingeraftekening is een halve eenheid.
Wanneer de handen op een donker achtergrond afgebeeld worden dienen zij door een witte lijn van een dikte van één eenheid afgetekend te worden.
De kleuren van de hand zijn op basis van de referenties PMS vastgesteld. Die norm zal altijd gebruikt worden wat het realisatieproces van de signaletische elementen ook moge zijn, behalve de vierkleurendruk waardoor die kleuren opnieuw gecreëerd kunnen worden.

SIGNALETIQUE
La main:
description, couleurs

Autour de l'emblème s'articule un système de signalisation basé sur la symbolique de la main. Ce système se décline des sept façons illustrées ci-contre et en page suivante. Ces éléments seront utilisés tant à l'extérieur qu'à l'intérieur des points de vente. L'épaisseur du contour des doigts est d'une demi-unité. Quand les mains sont appliquées sur un fond sombre, elles sont serties dans un filet blanc dont l'épaisseur est d'une unité.
Les couleurs de la main ont été déterminées sur base des références PMS. Cette norme sera utilisée quel que soit le procédé adopté pour la réalisation des éléments signalétiques, excepté la quadrichromie pour laquelle ces tons peuvent être recréés.

Kleur van het embleem
Couleur de l'emblème

De kleur van het embleem is blauw PMS 534. Het levis logo is wit. De PMS 534 kan in vierkleurendruk gereproduceerd worden.
Als het embleem in een 1-kleurendruk op een gekleurde achtergrond moet geplaatst worden dient wit gebruikt te worden voor de vijfhoek, het logo (Levis) blijft dan in de kleur van de ondergrond (b.v.: ballonnetjes).

De betrouwbaarheid van de courante kleurstalen blijkt niet steeds te voldoen, daarom is het aangewezen de stalen van het normalisatie handboek als referentie te gebruiken. Door het aanpassen van de basissamenstelling kan men dan zo tot de juiste inktsamenstelling komen.

La couleur de l'emblème est le bleu PMS 534. Le logo Levis est blanc. Le PMS 534 peut être reconstitué en quadrichromie.
Si l'emblème doit être appliqué sur un fond de couleur en un seul passage d'impression, on utilisera le blanc, le logo restant dans la couleur du support (exemple: ballonnets).

La fiabilité des nuanciers habituellement utilisés n'étant pas suffisante, on se référera dans tous les cas aux échantillons de couleurs du manuel de normalisation pour la reconstitution des encres, en "ajustant" la composition de base.

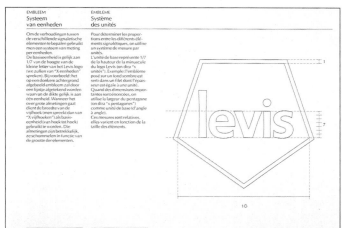

Systeem van eenheden
Système des unités

Om de verhoudingen tussen de verschillende signaletische elementen te bepalen gebruikt men een systeem van meting met eenheden.
De basiseenheid is gelijk aan 1/7 van de hoogte van de kleine letter van het Levis logo (we zullen van "X eenheden" spreken). Bij voorbeeld: het op een donkere achtergrond afgebeeld embleem zal door een lijntje afgetekend worden waarvan de dikte gelijk is aan één eenheid. Wanneer het over grote afmetingen gaat dient de breedte van de vijfhoek (men spreekt dan van "X vijfhoeken") als basiseenheid (van hoek tot hoek) gebruikt te worden. Die afmetingen zijn betrekkelijk, ze schommelen in functie van de grootte der elementen.

Pour déterminer les proportions entre les différents éléments signalétiques, on utilise un système de mesure par unités.
L'unité de base représente 1/7 de la hauteur de la minuscule du logo Levis (on dira "x unités"). Exemple: l'emblème posé sur un fond sombre est serti dans un filet dont l'épaisseur est égale à une unité. Quand des dimensions importantes sont énoncées, on utilise la largeur du pentagone (on dira "x pentagones") comme unité de base (d'angle à angle). Ces mesures sont relatives, elles varient en fonction de la taille des éléments.

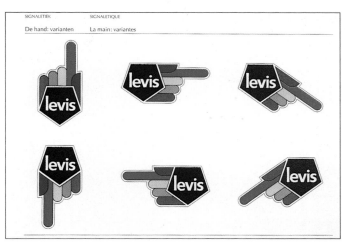

Fries: frekwentie der tekens (II)
Frise: fréquence des signes (II)

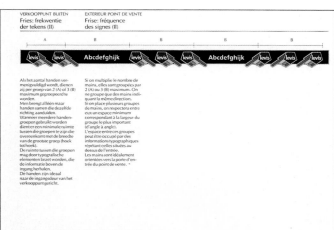

Als het aantal handen vermenigvuldigd wordt, dienen zij per groep van 2 (A) of 3 (B) maximum gegroepeerd te worden.
Men brengt alléén maar handen samen die dezelfde richting aanduiden.
Wanneer meerdere handengroepen gebruikt worden dient er een minimale ruimte tussen die groepen te zijn die overeenkomt met de breedte van de grootste groep (hoek tot hoek).
De ruimte tussen die groepen mag door typografische elementen bezet worden, die de informatie boven de ingang herhalen.
De handen zijn ideaal naar de ingangsdeur van het verkooppunt gericht.

Si on multiplie le nombre de mains, elles sont groupées par 2 (A) ou 3 (B) maximum. On ne groupe que des mains indiquant la même direction.
Si on place plusieurs groupes de mains, on respectera entre eux un espace minimum correspondant à la largeur du groupe le plus important (d'angle à angle).
L'espace entre ces groupes peut être occupé par des informations typographiques répétant celles situées au dessus de l'entrée.
Les mains sont idéalement orientées vers la porte d'entrée du point de vente.

De hand: varianten
La main: variantes

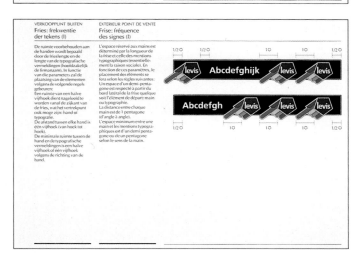

Fries: frekwentie der tekens (I)
Frise: fréquence des signes (I)

De ruimte voorbehouden aan de handen wordt bepaald door de trieslengte en de lengte van de typografische vermeldingen (hoofdzakelijk de firmanaam). In functie van die parameters zal de plaatsing van de elementen volgens de volgende regels gebeuren:
Een ruimte van een halve vijfhoek dient nageleefd te worden vanaf de zijkant van de fries, wat het vertrekpunt ook moge zijn: hand of typografie.
De afstand tussen elke hand is één vijfhoek (van hoek tot hoek).
De minimale ruimte tussen de hand en de typografische vermeldingen is een halve vijfhoek of één vijfhoek volgens de richting van de hand.

L'espace réservé aux mains est déterminé par la longueur de la frise et celle des mentions typographiques (essentiellement la raison sociale). En fonction de ces paramètres, le placement des éléments se fera selon les règles suivantes:
Un espace d'un demi-pentagone est respecté à partir du bord latéral de la frise quelque soit l'élément de départ: main ou typographie.
La distance entre chaque main est de 1 pentagone (d'angle à angle).
L'espace minimum entre une main et les mentions typographiques est d'un demi-pentagone ou d'un pentagone selon le sens de la main.

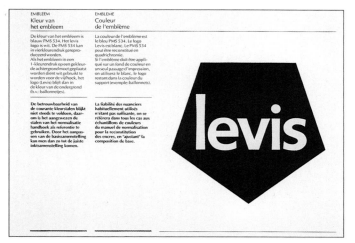

Bestelwagens
Camionnettes

hoogte van de typografie van het adres is gelijk aan 3/4 van die van de naam. Die vermeldingen zijn gecentreerd qua zetwerk en plaatsing.
Wanneer de oppervlakte van de carrosserie aan de voorkant van het voertuig groot genoeg is, kan de hand daar aangebracht worden met inachtneming van dezelfde regels als voor de andere gedeelten van het voertuig.

de 3/4 de celle du nom. Ces mentions sont centrées dans leur composition et leur placement.
Si la surface de carrosserie de l'avant du véhicule est suffisante, la main peut y être appliquée en respectant les mêmes règles d'encombrement que sur les autres parties du véhicules.

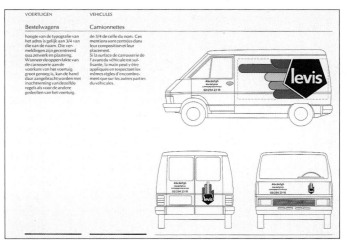

DENMARK

UNITED KINGDOM

GERMANY

IRELAND

LUXEMBOURG

NETHERLANDS

GREECE

BELGIUM

ITALY

FRANCE

SPAIN

PORTUGAL

Alan Fletcher

Alan Fletcher trained at the Royal College of Art in London and the School of Architecture and Design at Yale University. He began his career in New York where he worked for the Container Corporation, Fortune Magazine and IBM. Moving to London in 1959, he co-founded Fletcher/Forbes/Gill which served such clients as Pirelli, Cunard, Olivetti and Reuters.

Founder member of Pentagram in 1972, his clients have included IBM Europe, the Mandarin Oriental Hotel Group, Lloyd's of London, and Scandinavian Airlines. He is consultant to OUN International, Tokyo. Fletcher has received gold awards from the British Designers & Art Directors Association, and the New York 'One Show'. In 1977 he shared with Colin Forbes, a Pentagram partner based in New York, the Designers & Art Directors Association President's Award for outstanding contributions to design. In 1982, the Society of Industrial Artists and Designers awarded him the Annual Medal for outstanding achievement in industrial design. He is Royal Designer for Industry, a Fellow of the Chartered Society of Designers, and a Senior Fellow of the Royal College of Art. Fletcher has had the honour of being president of the Designers & Art Directors Association, and international president of the Alliance Graphique Internationale.

Among the books Fletcher has co-authored are 'Identity Kits - a pictorial survey of visual signs', 'Graphic Design - a visual comparison', 'A Sign Systems Manual', and two publications on the work of Pentagram, 'Living by Design' and 'Ideas on Design'.

Design is what happens between conceiving an idea and the fashioning of the means to carry it out - whether the big stuff like painting a picture, composing an opera, writing a novel, conducting a military battle, or running a commercial enterprise or even a smaller task like reorganising a room. A few people also earn their living giving form to the amenities of life in the context of manufacturing, communication or place. They call themselves designers. Designers are artists who occupy themselves solving other people's problems. Actually that's an oversimplification. The real issue is the elegance of the solution. And that always leads to an intimate confrontation because it is more of a personal challenge than utilitarian discipline, a commitment rather than an involvement much like ham and eggs - the pig is totally committed but the chicken is merely involved.

Anyway, designers derive their rewards from inner standards of excellence, from the intrinsic satisfaction of their tasks. They are committed to the task not the job, to their standards not their bosses. So whereas some people's lives are divided between time spent earning money, and time spending it, designers generally lead a seamless existence in which work and play are synonymous. As a designer, I never work - all the time.

Trying to describe how to ride a bicycle is notoriously difficult, and the same distance lies between experience and theory in trying to describe the design process. To my mind the current practice of defining design as 'problem solving' smacks more of routine work than creative thinking. In reality, designers are committed to challenging situations where they can play with problems, and since that is a personal game, if someone asks a designer how he came up with an idea, he'll probably say what he thinks you expect to hear: anything from "it just popped into my head" to "it was a mystical experience involving levitating llamas." For myself I try to sum up the situation, back in edgeways, and cast around for ideas on which to hang further ideas. It's an intuitive process involving search, discovery, recognition, evaluation, and rejection of development. There are no specific rules or recipes; one might slip through a sequence of actions in seconds, or sweat through step by step. Start backwards, move randomly from one point to another, or do what the surf riders call 'hang ten'. Get your toes into the board and ride the waves.

There is a sequence in solving a problem. It's much like the game Snakes and Ladders. The initial move is getting the bits and pieces into some kind of order to point up the problem. The next move is to head off along the most likely route. The solution may be instantly evident, or lead to an exasperating period of hiatus when despite trying this and that the answer still remains elusive. Hopefully the germ of an idea will eventually peep through, but before leaping on it with relief, let it incubate for a while. Here the mind works in some mysterious way and either the idea's potential evaporates (in which case one has to start all over again) or it emerges with "a firm iridescent surface, and a notable increase in weight" (Henry James).

Whatever the personal recipe, whatever the personal rules of process there is one essential condition all design artists must have. They must have the capability for cerebral acrobatics so that the mind can juggle the elements while freewheeling around the possibilities. A mind set which has the credulity of a child, the dedication of an evangelist, and the spadework of a navvy will reach a "condensation of sensation" that the artist Matisse said, "constitutes a picture."

The National Portrait
Gallery

*The National Portrait
Gallery commissioned
Pentagram to design a
poster to promote its new
20th century galleries. As
the Gallery is concerned
more with portraits of
famous people than with
portraits by famous
artists, the poster was
designed to emphasise*
*this popular appeal.
Pentagram took an
informal approach
using a typewriter for
the copy and a very
recognisable personality
as a central image. The
picture of the Prince is a
composite of extracts
from a number of
different portraits in the
Gallery collection.*

Portraits of famous British Personalities
from 1945 to the 1990's are on permanent
exhibition at the 20th Century Galleries
in the National Portrait Gallery.
Free admission. Open 10 to 5pm weekdays,
10 to 6pm Saturdays and 2 to 6pm Sundays.
Nearest ⊖ Leicester Square & Charing Cross

**IBM Charitable
Contribution Campaign**

*Two of a series of ten
posters designed for an
annual IBM social
programme. The purpose
was to encourage IBM
employees to contribute
to charity.
(Designers: Alan Fletcher,
Debbie Martindale, Nick
Simmons)*

SEITA

*Gitanes commissioned a
number of inter-
nationally recognised
designers to produce
posters for a promotional
touring exhibition. Alan
Fletcher's poster pays
homage to Max Ponty
who designed the original
gypsy for Gitanes
cigarettes in the 1950s.*

a homage to Max Ponty

**Pentagram/Design
Museum**

*A poster to promote the
first annual Pentagram
Lecture held at the Design
Museum. The speaker for
this occasion was the
Italian architect/product
designer, Mario Bellini.
(Designers: Alan Fletcher,
Eamon Brennan)*

MARIO BELLINI,
ARCHITECT/DESIGNER
GIVES THE FIRST ANNUAL
PENTAGRAM LECTURE. THE
DESIGN MUSEUM 22 MAY 1991.
WEDNESDAY FROM 7.30 TO 9PM.
TICKETS £10, CONCESSIONS £7.50,
FROM THE DESIGN MUSEUM
BUTLERS WHARF, LONDON
SE1 2YD. TELEPHONE:
071 403 6933 BETWEEN
9.30/5.30 WEEKDAYS,
OR FAX 071 378 6540.
MARIO BELLINI IS
AN ARCHITECT AND
PRODUCT DESIGNER OF
ENORMOUS RANGE AND VARIETY:
THE TOKYO DESIGN CENTRE, A MAJOR
EXPANSION OF THE SITE OF THE MILAN FAIR.
THE CAB CHAIR FOR CASSINA. THE PERSONA AND
FIGURA OFFICE CHAIRS FOR VITRA. THE DIVISUMMA
LOGOS CALCULATORS AND THE ETP 55 TYPEWRITER
FOR OLIVETTI, FOR WHOM HE HAS BEEN CONSULTANT
SINCE 1962. MEMBER OF THE EXECUTIVE COMMITTEE
OF THE MILAN TRIENNALE IN 1986. PLANNED THE HUGE
PROGETTO DOMESTICO EXHIBITION. EDITOR OF DOMUS.
HE HAS WON NUMEROUS AWARDS: THE COMPASSO D'ORO
IN ITALY, THE ANNUAL AWARD IN THE USA, THE MADE IN
GERMANY AWARD, THE GOLD MEDAL IN SPAIN. TWENTY
OF HIS DESIGNS ARE IN THE PERMANENT COLLECTION OF
THE MUSEUM OF MODERN ART IN NEW YORK, WHERE AN
EXHIBITION DEVOTED TO HIS WORK WAS HELD IN 1987.

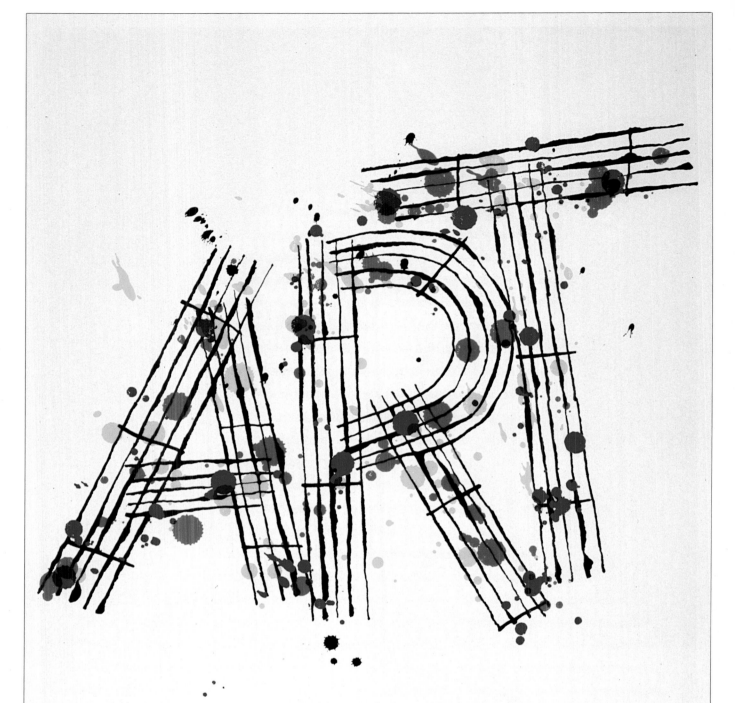

"All art constantly aspires
towards the condition
of music". Walter Pater

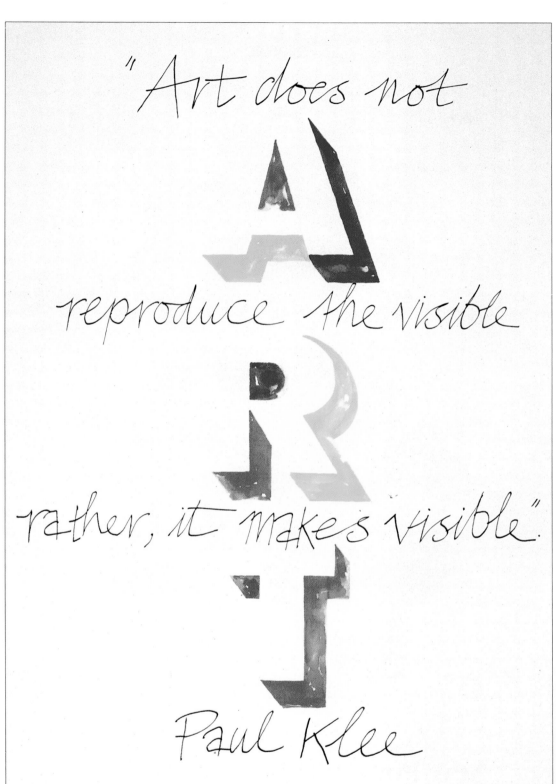

"Art does not reproduce the visible rather, it makes visible".

Paul Klee

IBM Europe

Two of a series of 6 posters to enliven the bare walls of IBM Europe's new headquarters in Tour Pascal, Paris when their extensive art programme fell behind schedule. The posters were designed around the word ART with the graphic image keyed to quotations from writers and artists. (Designers: Alan Fletcher, Tessa Boo Mitford)

Polaroid

Pentagram, in conjunction with advertising agents Ogilvy and Mather, created an advertising campaign to launch Polaroid's new Impulse Camera and 600 Image film. Pentagram selected, briefed and co-ordinated 18 designers of international standing to produce a series of bright, modern posters. The campaign appeared on outdoor billboard sites and in magazines advertising throughout Europe, followed by a book and a portfolio of limited edition prints.

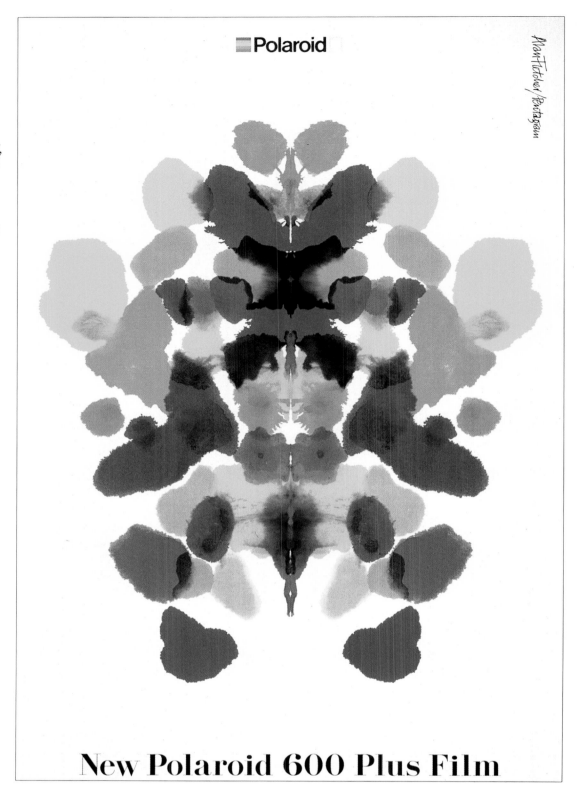

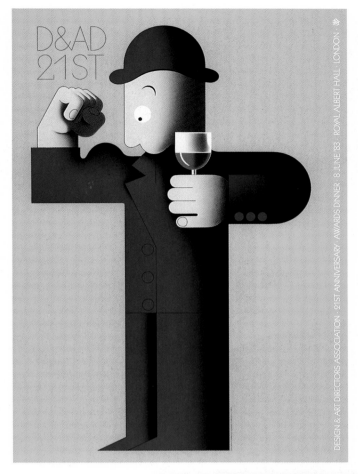

Designers & Art Directors Association

A poster for the 21st Birthday celebrations of the Association in London. The image was derived from one of Cassandre's famous advertisements for Dubonnet which appeared in 1933. The man originally wore a bathing costume but the addition of a blue suit made him a more suitable figure for the event. The design was also used as the image for invitations, menus, tickets and stationery for D&AD's anniversary dinner.

G & B Arts/Pentagram

G & B Arts is a silk screen printer. One of a series of posters to promote the company's services based on visual interpretations of famous quotations.

ICOGRADA

A poster for the 17th Icograda Student Seminar. The seminar comprises slide lectures by prominent international designers. The image was also used on the programme and admission tickets.

Lloyd's of London

Lloyd's of London is the centre of the international insurance market. In 1986, Pentagram was commissioned to design the signs for their new headquarters.

The programme included a large granite marker in Lime Street, a variety of special signs in the complex as well as the standard direction, information, identification and statutory signs.

Using a stencil alphabet by the architect/designer Le Corbusier, Pentagram developed a system that would complement the innovative architecture by Richard Rogers. Pentagram's system was precision-engineered, with each letter and number laser cut out of aluminium panels which were stove enamelled in primary colours.

Following the successful completion of the sign system, Pentagram was asked to undertake further commissions for Lloyd's including a commemorative album for the opening of the building and a collective identity for the corporation. (Designers: Alan Fletcher, Nick Simmons)

Victoria & Albert
Museum

The Victoria & Albert Museum is Britain's national museum of applied art and design. The logotype for the museum uses the original 18th century typeface of Giambattista Bodoni. The design utilises the ampersand to replace the cross bar of the 'A' which invests the mark with its distinctive personality.

The Museum houses the finest collection of its kind. The building itself has been added to many times since its opening of 1852 and is a complex maze of galleries and architectural styles. The Trustees approached Pentagram to design a sign system which would guide visitors through this often confusing building.

Pentagram's solution lay in a sign programme based on a colour compass; red for north, green for south, blue for west and yellow for east. Colour-coded fabric banners suspended at the entrance to each gallery carry the name of the exhibition(s) in a typeface designed in the 18th century by Bodoni. These link with a colour-coded map given to visitors when they enter the museum. (Designers: Alan Fletcher, Quentin Newark)

V&A

Alan Fletcher

A pair of metal gates, 2.5 metres high, constructed from the alphabet. The hinges carry the letters, the Q forms the gate stop. Moholy Nagy provides the scale. (Designers: Alan Fletcher, Pedro Guedes)

Expo-Vienna AG

The 1995 World's Fair, to be held in Vienna and Budapest, is the first Expo to be hosted by two cities and in two countries simultaneously.

Pentagram's symbol for the event was selected by an international jury of graphic designers in December 1990. It will act as the trademark and marketing symbol for the exposition and expresses the Expo 95 theme of "Bridges to the Future". (Designers: Alan Fletcher, Thomas Manss)

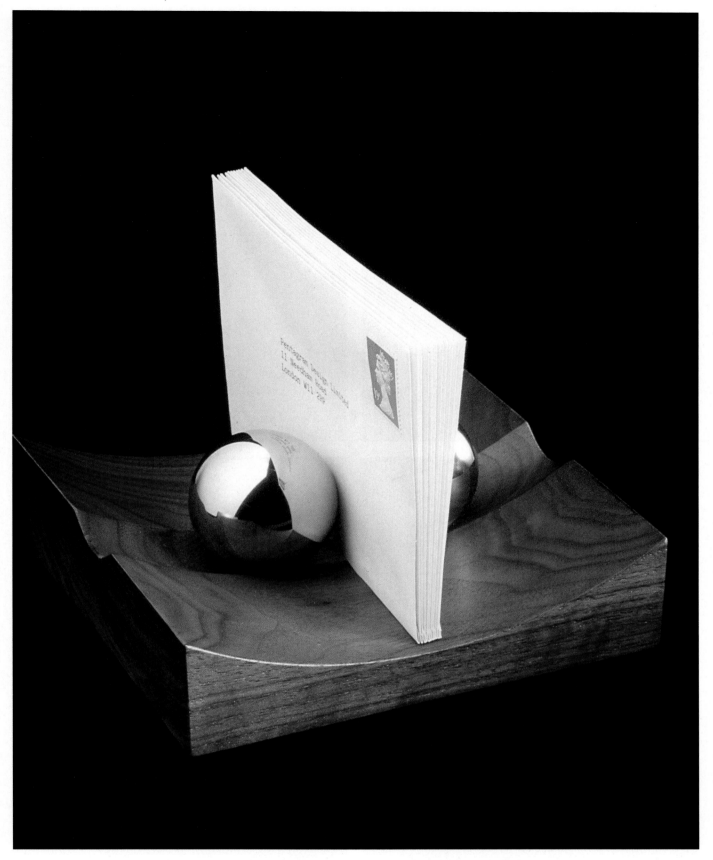

OUN International

The 'OUN Collection' is a range of unique design products devised by OUN International based in Tokyo. Alan Fletcher, Massimo Vignelli and Takenobu Igarashi are their international consultants.

This envelope holder has two chrome plated steel balls which sit on a mahogany base. Alan named it after his friend Massimo Vignelli. (Designers: Alan Fletcher, Penny Howarth)

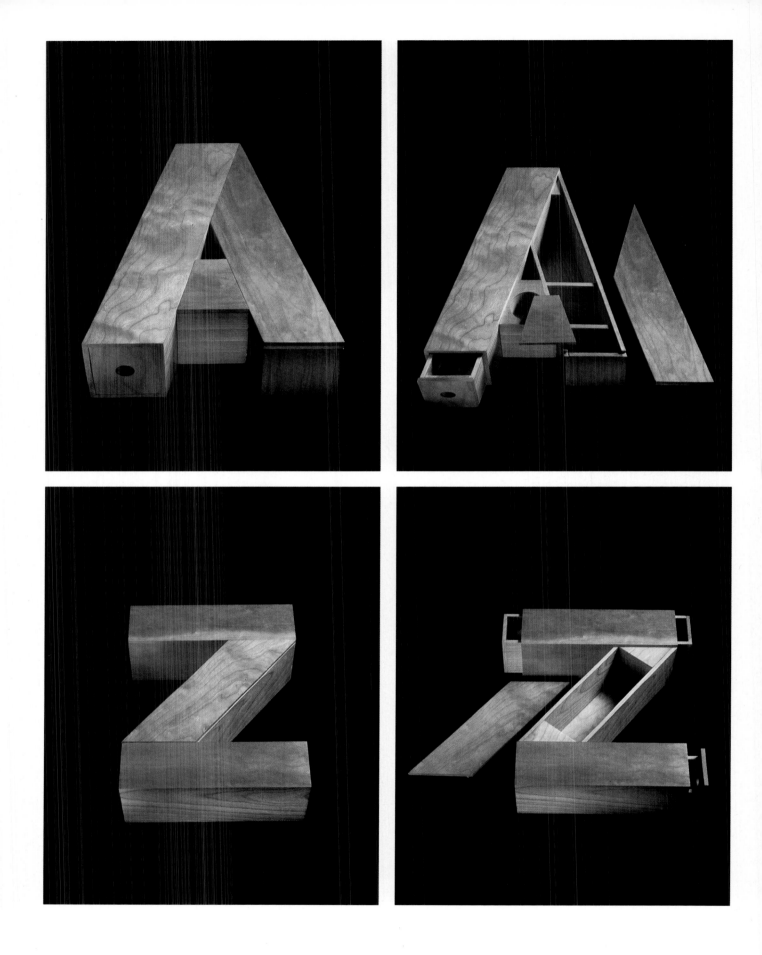

Pentagram

'Letterboxes' were created from the alphabet and numbers. Crafted in cherrywood, each has all sorts of little drawers, lids and panels to store small items.

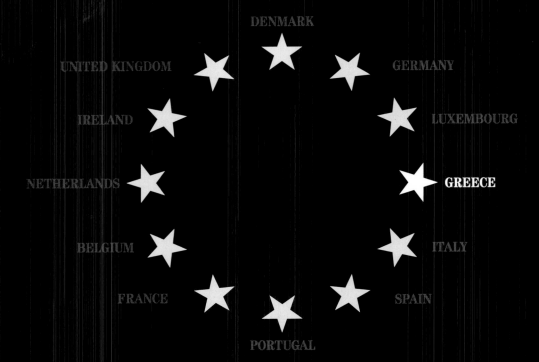

Michael Katzourakis

Michael Katzourakis was born in 1933 in Greece. His studies in Graphic Design took him to Paris where he spent four years studying painting under Andre Lhote and poster design in Paul Colin's studio. After returning to Athens, Katzourakis' freelance work rapidly achieved recognition. During the 1960's he was retained as design consultant to the Greek National Tourist Organisation and co-founded K & K Advertising. In 1973 he and his wife, Agni, who is also a designer, formed their own firm A & M Katzourakis which has concentrated on interior and graphic design in environmental projects, and is an acknowledged leader in the design of cruise ships. The Katzourakis team has worked on 35 passenger ships and their projects span into design on public buildings, institutions, and cultural events.

His graphic design work has been featured in many international publications and has won numerous awards, including seven Rizzoli Awards for best Greek advertisement, an honourable mention by the Art Director's Club of New York, a third prize at the Brno Biennale and first and second prizes in consecutive years at the Livorno International Tourist Poster Competition. In 1965, he was awarded the Golden Cross of the Order of the Phoenix for his outstanding contribution to Greek design, and since 1969 he has been an elected member of the Alliance Graphique Internationale (AGI).

Despite a busy designing schedule, Michael still sees painting as his vocation and is a highly active artist. His private work has been exhibited in numerous one-man and group shows in Greece and around the world.

Michael Katzourakis

Michael Katzourakis has the artistic creativity of image and variety but finds himself equally at ease in the field of environmental design which conforms to specific managerial and technological demands. Katzourakis prefers to stress the commonalities rather than the differences between the two activities, he believes both processes address a similar array of problems and utilise closely related sets of principles. His consistent involvement throughout the years with abstract geometry as a communicative medium facilitates and confirms the smooth transition from art to design.

In his work, the emphasis on abstraction is actually triggered by the direct stimuli of his environment. The use of rich primary colours and multiple dimensions is based on the design principle of repetitive patterns, where a design introduces a limitless unfolding of variations on a theme. It is a time honoured method used in certain oriental cultures where abstract geometry has direct affinities to industrial production processes and contemporary design. Katzourakis excels in taking this concept one step further, beyond the conventional use of it in modular units, and incorporates it into textures, colours, and a wide spectrum of interior spaces. He has changed the language but the guiding principle remains constant.

New trends in the international market, the evolving focus of safety regulations, and the ever shifting preferences of clients trying to keep abreast of fierce competition, are the diverse sources which have helped Katzourakis to expand on his creative talent. He rises above the definition of design as rational problem solving procedure and does not limit his work to mere functional needs, as is evidenced by his work in the area of cruise ship interiors. Compactly built interiors, which are used to transport one to a make-believe world, are easy targets for fanciful excesses. Katzourakis, however, chooses to lead in the opposite direction -one of restraint defined by elegance and serenity. His design, like his art, has developed novel approaches to materials and textures by focusing on the tactile qualities of natural and man-made structures. To the unobservant, his work may appear distant or ethereal, but it is in fact, firmly founded in this world which is Katzourakis' inspiration.

Mosaic mural at a mosque in Dubai

Carpet design

Detail of mosaic mural

MV Crown Odyssey

Top of the Crown/Bar

Galleria (entrance to restaurant)

MV Crown Odyssey

Top of the Crown/Dance floor with skylight

MV Horizon

*Side view of Horizon
Lobby*

*Rendez-Vous Lounge
(corridor to Cardroom
and Library)*

*General view of Horizon
Lobby*

MV Golden Odyssey

Stairtowers, laminated murals

Foyer with stained mirrors

Reliefs and sculptures

Vacuum formed
polystyrene sheets,
fluorescent colours

Sculpture
(painted wood)

Sculpture
(painted plywood)

Mitera Maternity Hospital
Corridors with entrances to wards (colour coding by floor)

MV Danae
Mural at half-landing, engraved and painted polyester

*Entrance to an
apartment building in
Athens*

Painting

Mixed media on limestone

Cover

Catalogue - M. Katzourakis
One Man Show

Painting

*Mixed media on cotton
duck*

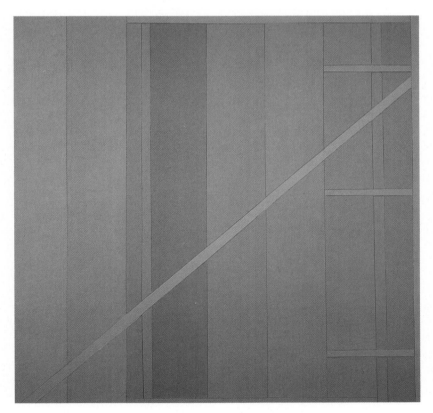

Painting

*Mixed media on cotton
duck*

DENMARK

UNITED KINGDOM

GERMANY

IRELAND

LUXEMBOURG

NETHERLANDS

GREECE

BELGIUM

ITALY

FRANCE

SPAIN

PORTUGAL

Italo Lupi

Graduate in Architecture from the Polytechnic of Milan, member of AGI (Alliance Graphique Internationale), Lupi has worked in the field of graphic design since 1972. He was Art Director of Domus, Rivista IBM, and the magazines 'Abitare', 'Shop', and 'Zodiac', and has been the designer of many other periodicals including 'Pubblicita Domani', and 'Contretemps' a Paris literary magazine. In 1992 Lupi accepted the position of Art Director and Editor of 'Abitare'. Lupi's varied graphic design talents have been used in private firms, publishing houses, enterprises of a social and political nature, museums, and scenery for television.

In collaboration with the architect Guido Canali he designed the layout of the exhibition '18th Century in Parma' in the Palazzo della Pinacoteca, and was co-designer of architectural design for the International Exhibition of the XVII Milan Triennale. Lupi's commissions include the signing systems for Light Railway Line in Milan, the 'Parchi Regionali Lombardi', the Tokyo Design Center, and new graphic images for the International Design Conference of Aspen (Colorado), the municipality of Chiba in Tokyo, and the Museo Poldi Pezzoli di Milano.

In 1990, he designed the graphic and signing system for the Italian cruise ship 'Costa Marina.' Lupi has won first prize from the Art Director's Club of Milan for editorial graphics, special mention at Typodomus in Prague, Silver Medal at the XIII International Graphics Biennale of Brno and was awarded a prize for one of his posters at the Lahti Biennale.

I work in the large, relaxing space of a renovated printing works building located in a historical part of Milan. The richness of space, a traditionally privileged city position, and a small staff of young, constructive assistants make my work conditions happy. I try and I hope that all of this feeling is in some way represented and poured into my work. Through my passion, curiosity, and practical experience, derived from my haunting of printing works, I got into graphic design shortly after graduating in Architecture. I have found that the training of an architect often adds to my way of dealing with the work I do now - its three dimensional vision contributes to not accepting the impositions and limits of the typographical cage. The attempt to translate a two dimensional into a three dimensional does not have to exclude the enrichment given from the infringement of rules; those rules serve to rationally channel the data of a project.

The power to pass from a poster (the work that I love the most for the synthetic application of all the elements of a problem) to a book or a commercial brochure, from an annual report to the complexity of a layout for a whole magazine, and from all that to an architectural project for a museum or exhibition, makes our trade absolutely fascinating. Like the historical part of Milan I work in, to make memories live in every new work without them becoming an obstruction, but to recognise them as the substantial base for new linguistics, is true graphic vitality. And love -love that is at the same time for modernism and for neo-classicism, for the hedonism and morality, for the eclecticism and versatility. These may be defects or contradictory but they allow graphic design to transform, maybe into art, maybe not, but most certainly into communication.

Poster

*Italian fashion
exhibition in New York*

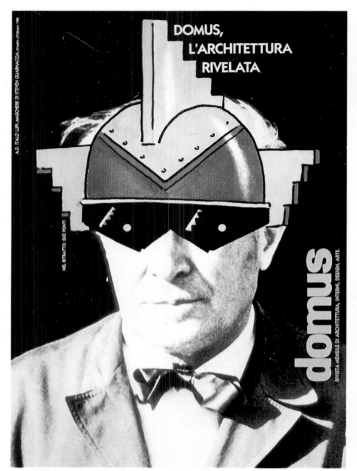

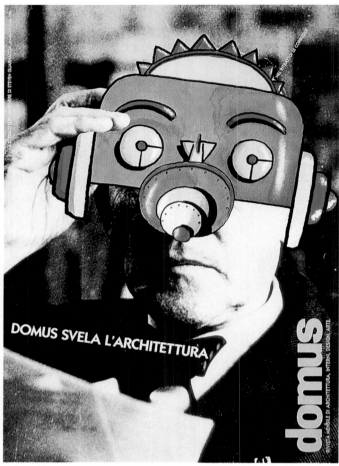

Posters

Domus magazine

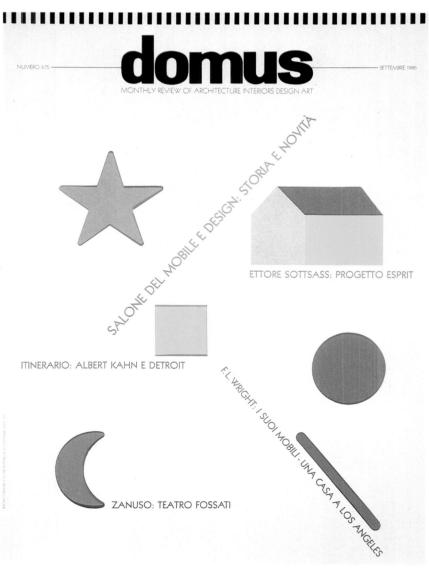

A.D. ITALO LUPI. MASCHERE DI STEVEN GUARNACCIA. Ottavia, LITORAMA, 1988

domus

RIVISTA MENSILE DI ARCHITETTURA, INTERNI, DESIGN, ARTE.

NEL RITRATTO: ALVAR AALTO

DOMUS SVELA IL DESIGN

A.D. ITALO LUPI. MASCHERE DI STEVEN GUARNACCIA. Ottavia, LITORAMA, 1988

domus

RIVISTA MENSILE DI ARCHITETTURA, INTERNI, DESIGN, ARTE.

NEL RITRATTO: L. MIES VAN DER ROHE

DOMUS IL DESIGN RIVELATO

domus

NUMERO 703 — MARZO 1989

MONTHLY REVIEW OF ARCHITECTURE INTERIORS DESIGN ART

Two covers of the magazines 'Domus' – the designs are cut-outs

TRIENNALE MUSEO IN PROGRESS

MILANO
PALAZZO DELL'ARTE
AL PARCO
ORARI:
FERIALE 16/20
SABATO E
FESTIVI 10/13 - 16/20
INGRESSO L. 1000

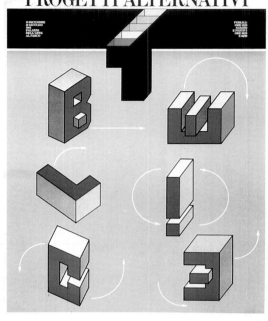

BELICE 1980
PROGETTI ALTERNATIVI

Le case della Triennale. Otto progetti di ambienti domestici contemporanei

XVI Triennale of Milan

*Poster and symbol (with
Alberto Maraugoni)*

*Poster for the project of
salvaging the areas of
Belice in Sicily,
damaged by earthquake*

Cover of a catalogue

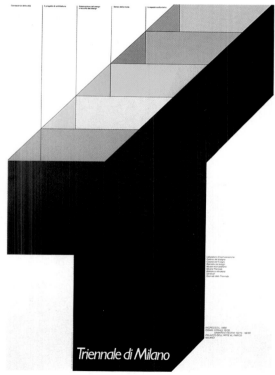

Triennale di Milano

LE CAS
E·DELL
A·TRIE
NNALE

I Quaderni della Triennale
ELECTA

Posters

*Two pieces for the XVII
Triennale of Milan*

*A convention for IBM
Italy in Vienna*

Posters

A series of conferences at the Architecture Museum of Frankfurt, Germany

Flos Lighting (design by Bau Scarabottolo)

The Poldi Pezzoli Museum

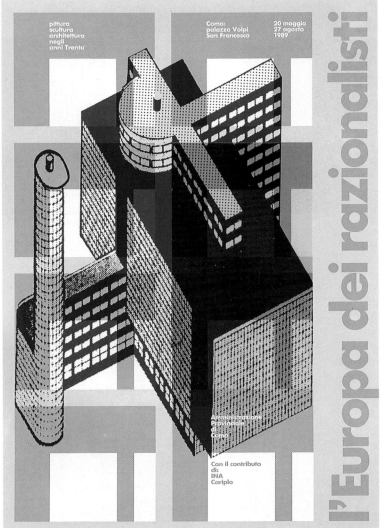

Posters

*The European
Telecommunications
Union on the occasion of
the 50th anniversary of
television in Europe*

*The restored National
Gallery of Parma*

*The European
Rationalism exhibition*

39TH INTERNATIONAL DESIGN CONFERENCE IN ASPEN, 13-18 JUNE 1989

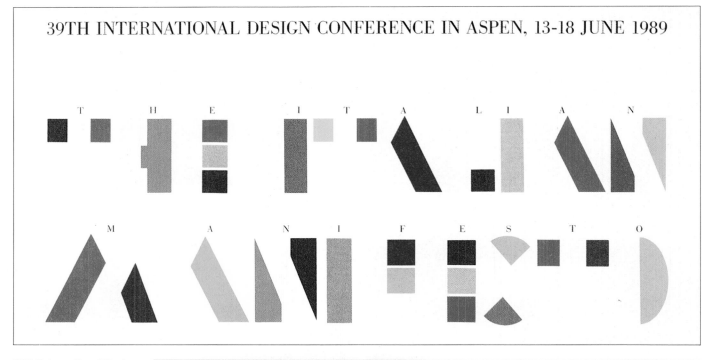

39th International Design
Conference in Aspen

Poster

Cover of brochure

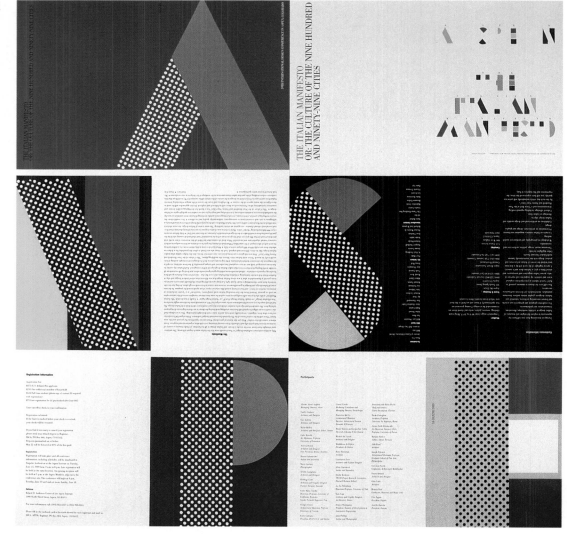

Covers

Abitare magazine

Luciano Benetton: la pubblicità non va mai tagliata

Ottanta miliardi spesi in advertising su un fatturato di 1700 miliardi.
La ricetta dell'azienda trevigiana è semplice.
Global marketing, strategie aggressive e acquisto spazi unificato.
Cresce però il marchio di nicchia.
Il gigante non può riposare.

LIA MEZZATESTA. «La nostra politica rispetto alla pubblicità e più in generale alla comunicazione è stata sicuramente uno dei fattori strategici di successo del gruppo. Accanto al prodotto, ovviamente, è alla forza distributiva». Così Luciano Benetton sintetizza per *Pubblicità Domani* il ruolo che l'advertising ha avuto nel successo del suo gruppo. «Abbiamo creduto fin dall'inizio in un approccio aggressivo, innovativo (linguaggio di Oliviero Toscani), e internazionale»

Queste scelte sono rimaste costanti mentre il gruppo, nel corso degli anni, ha cambiato pelle. Quando è nato non aveva praticamente stabilimenti e fondava il suo successo proprio sulla grande flessibilità dei fattori distributivi. Oggi ha 14 stabilimenti da cui escono ogni anno milioni di jeans, maglioni, camicette che riforniscono 5.500 negozi. C'è stata anche un'escursione nel campo della finanza che adesso è rientrata. Infatti l'amministratore delegato, Aldo Palmieri, l'uomo che aveva promosso questa diversificazione, è uscito dal gruppo. La scelta adesso è quella di concentrarsi soprattutto nell'industria facendo nascere, intorno alla fabbrica di sci Nordica un importante polo sportivo. Ed è indubbio che la pubblicità sarà uno degli elementi trainanti di questa nuova sfida. «Tradizionalmente -aggiunge Benetton- noi destiniamo alla comunicazione una quota pari al 4-4,5 per cento del fatturato» che nel 1989 ha raggiunto i 1.700 miliardi. La Benetton (primo utente di un paese capitalistico a pianificare sulla tv polacca) è una delle poche aziende italiane che ha scelto il global marketing. A differenza, per esempio, della Fiat i cui prodotti assumono, in ciascun Paese, valori molto diversi. Il messaggio che lancia è uguale in tutti i 40 Paesi in cui l'azienda trevigiana ha deciso di promuovere con forza i suoi prodotti. Si tratta, spesso, di una comunicazione puramente istituzionale. E la ragione di questa scelta è abbastanza semplice. La Benetton immette nel mercato ogni anno circa mille capi base. Ognuno viene realizzato con diverse tonalità di colore.

Vuol dire che, ogni sei mesi (collezioni di autunno-inverno e primavera-estate) ci sono diverse centinaia di nuove realizzazioni che vengono presentate sul mercato. In queste condizioni sarebbe assurdo promuovere un solo prodotto. Così si punta solo sull'headline che adesso è diventato addirittura un marchio (United Colors of Benetton). Una scelta impostata dal fatto che ogni negoziante, pur essendo libero di scegliere il suo target di utenti, è praticamente costretto a rimanere dentro una "linea" di collegamento con la casa madre di Treviso. Sul valore strategico della pubblicità il leader del gruppo trevigiano, naturalmente, non nutre alcun dubbio. È convinto, ad esempio che serva ad aumentare il volume complessivo dei consumi e non si limiti a spostarli da un prodotto all'altro: «**È un accumulo di esperienze che si fa con il tempo. I progetti vanno portati avanti negli anni e non solo quando le vendite cominciano a calare**». Per Luciano Benetton è un clamoroso errore tagliare gli investimenti quando l'impresa comincia a dare qualche segno di stanchezza. «**La pubblicità crea molto valore aggiunto**» dice. Questo ragionamento vale a maggior ragione quando ci si trova alle prese con un settore maturo come il tessile «dove l'innovazione-afferma-viaggia soprattutto sulle gambe dello stile e della comunicazione» Proprio per dimostrare questa sua fede incrollabile nella funzione dell'advertising si è offerto di fare da "testimonial" per la campagna promozionale per American Express «È stato un episodio simpatico» ricorda con una battuta). Il gruppo trevigiano è riuscito a trasformare la pubblicità in un piccolo business. L'ha intrapreso attraverso la monoposto di Formula 1 che porta il nome Benetton. Il team fu acquistato alla metà degli anni '80 come strumento di affermazione del marchio. Era un salto in avanti rispetto al passato, quando l'azienda si era limitata a sponsorizzare la Tyrrel prima e l'Alfa Romeo poi. Quindi acquistò un minuscolo team britannico e lo ribattezzò Benetton. «**Oggi** -dice Luciano- **la nostra monoposto è uno strumento molto potente di comunicazione assolutamente indispensabile per un gruppo che vuole avere una strategia mondiale. Oltre a "velocizzare" il marchio, questo mezzo si presta moltissimo per raggiungere i target più alti del mercato**». Il salto di qualità verrà effettuato nei prossimi anni quando la squadra manterrà il nome mentre gli spazi pubblicitari verranno venduti ad altre aziende intenzionate a far conoscere il loro nome nei quattro continenti dove si corrono le gare di Formula 1. Già oggi accanto al marchio Benetton figurano altri sponsor. Domani tutta la carrozzeria sarà "venduta" e il marchio trevigiano assumerà una funzione non diversa da quella che oggi hanno McLaren, Williams, Tyrrel e così via. In questa ottica di "globalizzazione" del business gli uomini di Treviso non sono affatto preoccupati del processo di concentrazione che mezzi e concessionarie stanno subendo in Italia dopo l'acquisto da parte della Fininvest di Silvio Berlusconi della Mondadori e della prevista interazione delle due concessionarie, la Publitalia e la Manzoni. «**Noi** -dice Luciano Benetton- **abbiamo un media-planning che abbraccia tutto il mondo e viene gestito dalla J. W. Thompson. Siamo presenti in quaranta Paesi e questo ci mette un pò al riparo dalle vicende italiane**» ⌐

Two pages from the magazine "Pubblicità Domani"

Cover for the magazine "Il giornale della Lombardia"

Cover for interior design magazine "Progex"

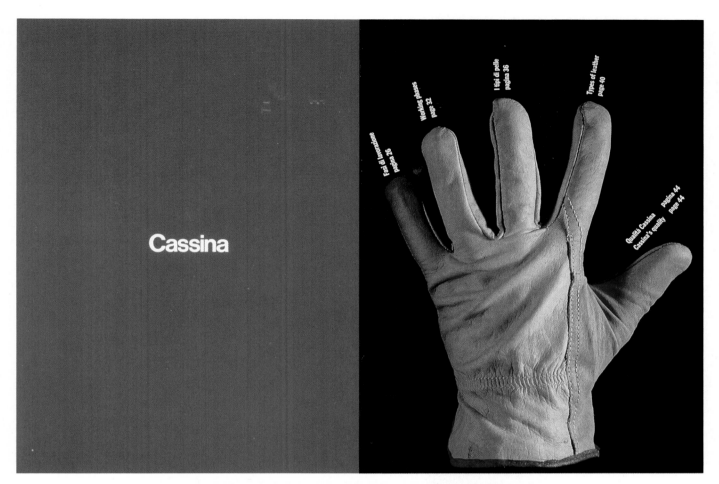

Cassina

Folder for Cassina (furnishings)

Annual report for IBM Italy

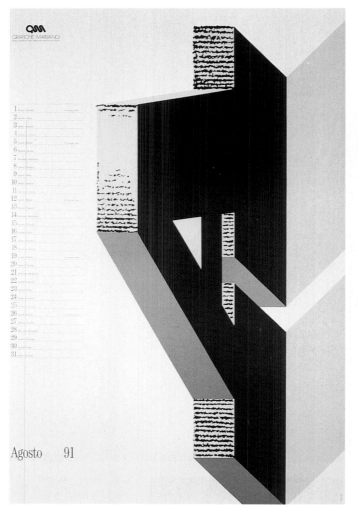

Page from a calendar

Cover for a calendar

Postcard for the AGI Congress in Oslo

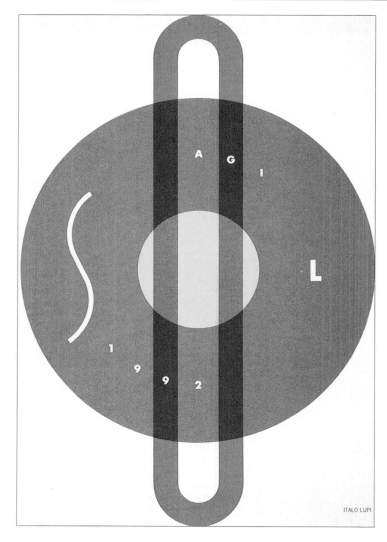

Pierre Mendell

Pierre Mendell was born in 1929 in Essen, Germany. In 1934 his family immigrated to France and thirteen years later immigrated once more to the United States. In 1953, Mendell returned to France and worked for a period in his family's texile factory and later studied at the School for Design in Basel, Switzerland under the direction of Armin Hofmann. In 1960 while working for Michael Engelmann, Mendell became acquainted with Klaus Oberer, and by 1961 they had formed the highly successful partnership of Studio Mendell & Oberer, which operates out of Munich.

Mendell's many accolades include the honour of being invited to return to the United States and lecture about his work and achievements at the 1982 International Design Conference in Aspen. Mendell is a member of both the Art Directors Club in Germany, and the Alliance Graphique Internationale.

The statement "advertising is art" is a view not shared by Pierre Mendell, despite the many awards and exhibitions that have recognised the artistic design of his work. Mendell insists that "Graphic design is not art, it is communication." Graphic design should raise attention, inform, and convince. It should persuade as many people as possible to buy a product, trust an enterprise, visit an exhibit or theatre performance, or support a social cause -it is a means to an end. Graphic design must be clear and unequivocal to be successful. Art, however, may be ambivalent and difficult to decipher. Graphic design must get the message across. Art may take the liberty of unveiling its secrets through interpretation. Graphic design must be understood by the general public. Art can afford to not appeal to the masses and direct itself to a select group of connoisseurs; an artist only has to express himself and his ideas. By contrast, a graphic designer is confronted with a mountain of specifications, objectives, constraints, and secondary considerations.

Pierre Mendell's work is characterized by a willingness to take the people seriously and not offend their intelligence. Looking around one sees the pollution of the visual environment which dulls the senses because too many designers and communicators do not care about those to whom their message is directed. Advertising and design companies too often equate the masses with low level intelligence and dullness, which is manifested by didactic messages in the work they produce. Mendell never lowers himself to the level of commands and monologues. Design communication to him is always a dialogue with a companion who happens to not be sitting on the other side of the work table. His work is a conversation, always conducted as it should be between cultivated people, clear and unequivocal, without shouting or chest-beating, and without lies. There is always something inspiring about his work, an intelligent joke, a new perspective, or a missing link which invites the viewer to participate. Mendell's best works are never blatantly explained. There is always a blank spot saved for the viewer's associations and imagination. The image supports the imagination.

Again and again Mendell successfully opens new perspectives by making the familiar look unfamiliar -an extremely difficult task in a world flooded with stimuli where everything seems repetitious and ordinary. Mendell's work makes the familiar look fresh with his creative solutions: the constricted balloon as a symbol for intestinal gas; the Libero logo for children's sport shoes, where the R kicks off the O like a defender in a soccer match. Powerful colours in the Mediterranean style, eye-winking humour, and esprit mark the work of Mendell which have been referred to as "visual haiku" because they jump straight to the subject and achieve the maximum effect in the shortest period of time. Such simplicity is not easy; it is brilliant.

(Pierre Mendell and Klaus Oberer, together, own the design company of Mendell and Oberer. The philosophical opinions and successes here are Oberer's as well.)

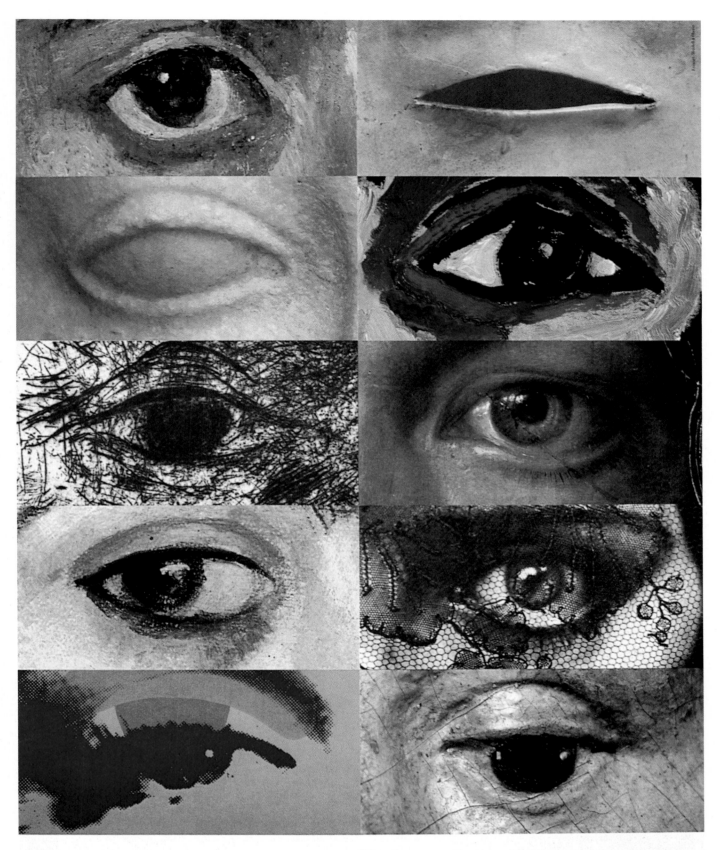

Kunst öffnet die Augen.

Besuchen Sie Bayerns Staatliche Museen.

Poster

Bavarian State Museum

Mendell & Oberer Graphic Design

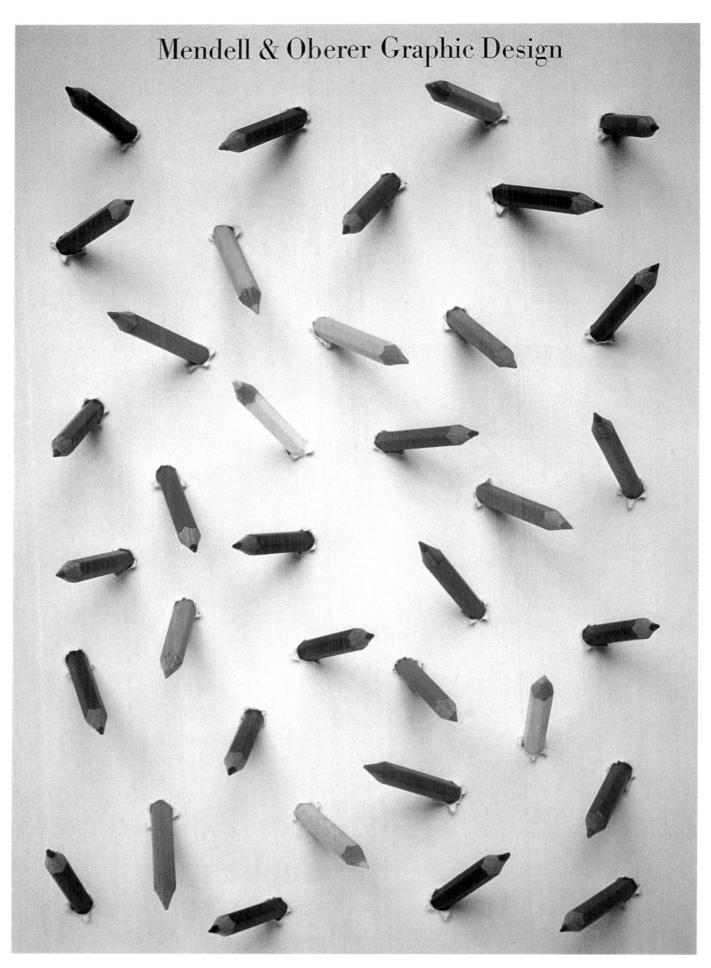

Poster

Mendell and Oberer

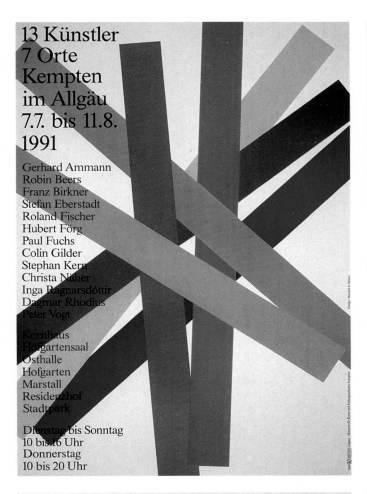

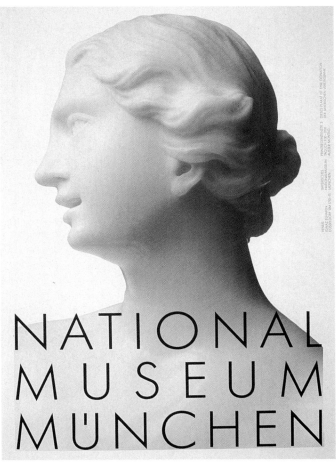

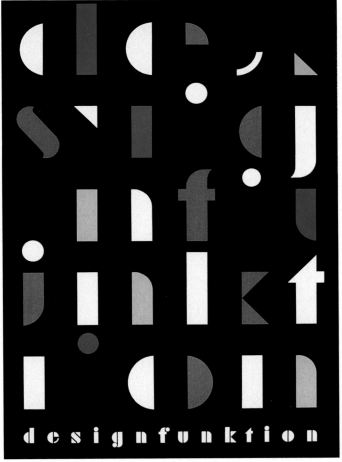

Collective art exhibition in Kempten, Germany

Opening of the Neve Pinakothek Museum in Münich

Bavarian National Museum in Münich

Furniture store

Posters

Posters for the Neve
Sammlung Museum

*Exhibit on the design
process of automobiles*

Neve Sammlung Museum
for applied art

Exhibit of Amish Quilts

"I Love Design"

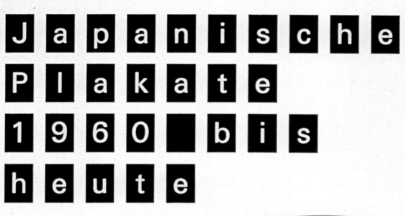

Japanische
Plakate
1960 bis
heute

26. Oktober 1988
bis 15. Januar 1989
Dienstag bis Sonntag
10 bis 17 Uhr
Die Neue Sammlung
Prinzregentenstrasse 3
München

Poster

*Exhibit of Japanese
posters at the Neve
Sammlung Museum*

Donationen
und Neu-
erwerbungen
1980–1981

Die Neue
Sammlung
Staatliches
Museum für
angewandte
Kunst

Hans Wichmann

Donationen und
Neuerwerbungen 1986/87

Industrial Design, Unikate,
Serienerzeugnisse

Die Neue Sammlung
Staatliches Museum
für angewandte Kunst
München

NEU

bahnbrecher hans gugelot 1920–1965
systemdesign

Walter Jens

Der Untergang

Kindler

Covers Catalogues of exhibits at
the Neve Sammlung
Museum

Book "Going Under" by
Walter Jens

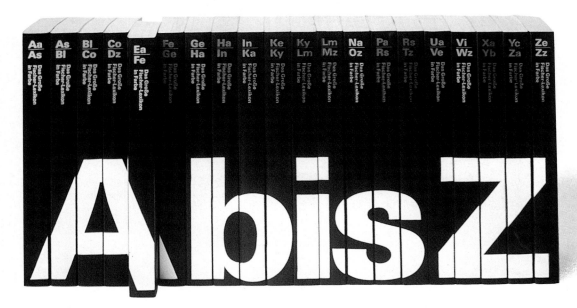

Covers

Dictionary

Book "Notes of a dirty old man" by Charles Bukowsky

Book on famous pianists

Shopping bags
Fashion store Harry's

*Fashion store Angela
Grashoff*

Sportswear store Unützer

*Logo, book and
magazine covers for the
Oldenbourg Publishing
Company*

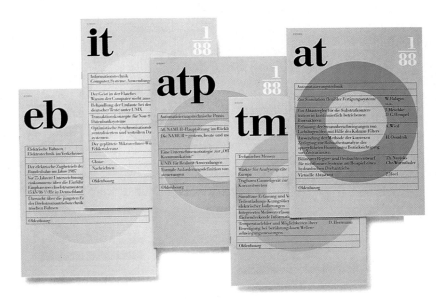

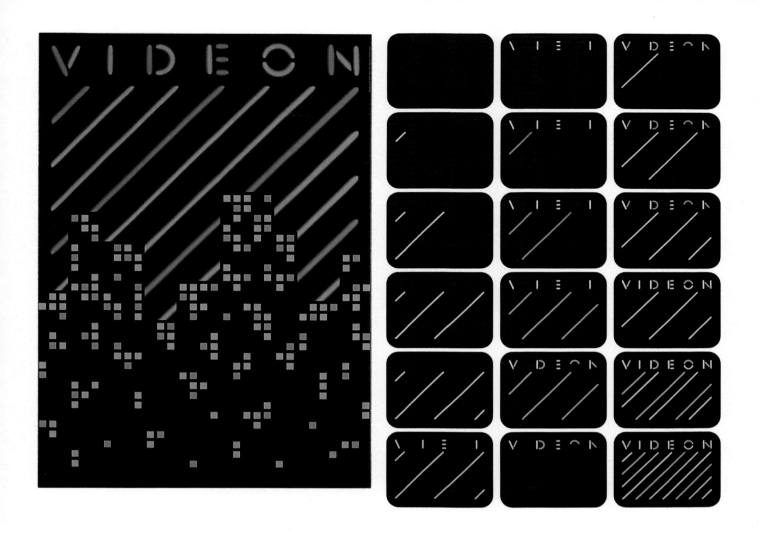

*Logo and corporate
identity manual for the
Kirch Group, movie film
distributors*

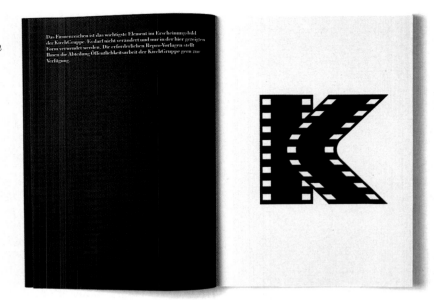

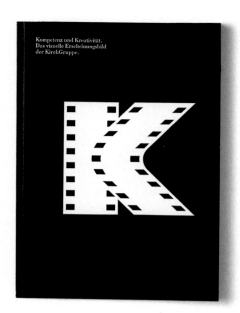

DENMARK

UNITED KINGDOM

GERMANY

IRELAND

LUXEMBOURG

NETHERLANDS

GREECE

BELGIUM

ITALY

FRANCE

SPAIN

PORTUGAL

Tony O'Hanlon

Tony O'Hanlon was born in 1948 in Cork, Ireland. As a student he studied architecture at Cork College of Art, and design at the London College of Printing. O'Hanlon has worked as a free-lance designer in London and as a lecturer at the Limerick College of Art and Design. From 1977 to 1986, O'Hanlon was a principal graphic designer of the famous Kilkenny Design Consultancy, which was responsible for giving Irish Design an international presence. He now works in Galway, Ireland, with the European Design Group of the Digital Equipment Corporation.

O'Hanlon is the recipient of several design awards, and winner of the international competition for the design symbol of the European Patent Organisation. He has adjudicated for Zgraf 6 (International Exhibition of Graphic Design and Communications), the international competition for the design of the European Currency 'the Ecu', the Digital Design Bursary, and the 'Kieler Woche' sailing festival in Kiel, Germany. His invitations have taken him to Munich for the 1992 International Litfass Art Biennale, and to Paris where he was one of twelve participating designers that worked on promotion activities for the signing of the European Act. Publications include: 'Graphis Annual' (Switzerland), 'Design' (UK), 'Mobelia' (Denmark), 'Modern Publicity' (UK),

'Trademarks and Symbols of the World' (Japan), and 'Novum Gebrauchs-graphik' (Germany).

Exhibitions of O'Hanlon's work have been mounted in Paris at 'The Art of the Poster' and The International Association of Art. His work has also appeared at The 1988 Lahti Poster Biennale, and the 1987 UNESCO Poster Exhibition in Amsterdam.

Implicit in the term 'Common Market Design' is the acceptance of a common identity or signature that transcends national boundaries, a trans-territorial economic community at peace, sharing the benefits of a rich cultural economic history.

One cannot help fearing that today's wide access to technology can cut short the gradual process which results in good design. This is especially true when cloning approaches have already proven successful and are increasingly used in the market place. Thus, many questions, which may have been asked in order to stimulate and leave the door open to the possibility of new and individual responses, are forfeited in favour of covering the same old ground. Clients now talk about their favourite typefaces, the language and technology is being used by all. Although in recent years there has been a gradual closing of the gap between the client and his/hers understanding of the technology associated with the design profession, the essence of design still remains illusive.

For the last few years I have been living in Galway, in the West of Ireland, working in the Corporate Design department of Digital Equipment. This provides an interesting paradox: to be living in a far corner of Europe, on the Atlantic seaboard, between the wild landscapes of Connemara and the Burren, and yet to be part of a high-tech worldwide corporation. To many designers, working on commercial projects in a large urban centre, this may seem like a side-step out of mainstream Graphic Design. The questions most frequently asked centre around two points: is there an opportunity for real design in a large corporation, and how can you work from a remote location?

Design work in a corporation? Well, we haven't abandoned traditional design; the studio produces all the usual annual reports, posters, marketing literature, etc. In addition, however, we can address some very fundamental problems of information design, and can do so in new and exciting ways. Information Technology is responsible for a great deal of the information overload and information pollution today but it can also provide the solution we need. Information Technology is a crucial place for today's Graphic Designer to be. Icon-based graphical interfaces, screen design, on-line tutorials, hypermedia with sound and animation -these are the logical extensions of the design arena. Working with these new media, in multi-discipline teams, with software engineering, human factors, industrial design, user publications, etc., the Graphic Designer has a critical role to play in creating the new generation of products and systems which will cause Information Technology to evolve into the understanding business. That is mainstream design in the 1990s.

As for being remote, we work every day with clients throughout Europe and North America. We do some travelling but mostly we use computer communications, satellite links, and FAX. Remoteness is not an issue in the electronic age; it is not even a meaningful concept. Who is remote from whom in this global village?

For the designer, the challenge remains to produce valid responses to the demands and problems of this age. Successful information design really wins when both the originator of the information and the designer understand the spirit of a text or a problem -the result is an unquestionable fusion of both. The understanding of communication is really the first step in the process of translating the intended spirit.

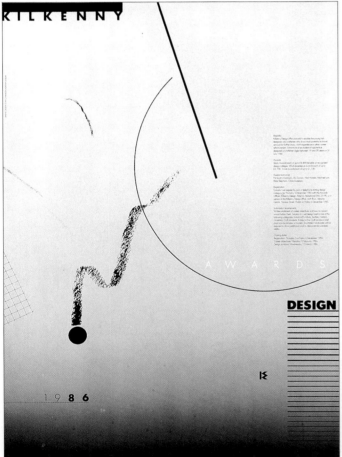

*'Call for entry' posters
for Kilkenny Design
Awards. An annual
student design event
aimed at assisting
graduates financially in*

*their search for work
experience and travel
awards.
Client: Kilkenny Design*

Vienna Boys Choir

St Canice's Cathedral
■ Kilkenny
Monday 23 November
8:00pm One performance
Tickets £5:00
Senior Citizens and
Students half price

Poster

Vienna Boys Choir
Client: Kilkenny Arts
Week

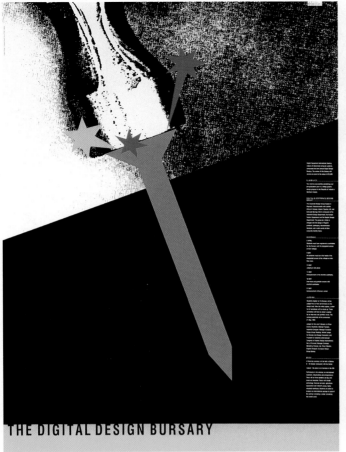

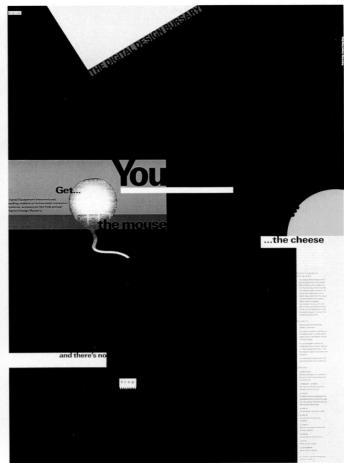

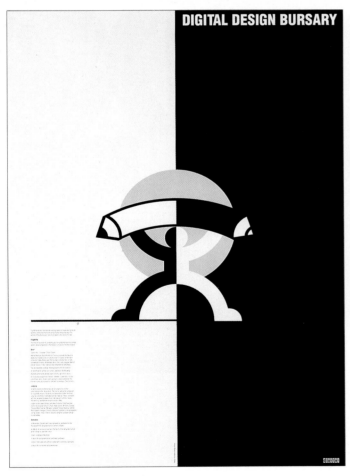

THE DIGITAL DESIGN BURSARY

DIGITAL DESIGN BURSARY

Europe

culture et communication

Poster submission for a design event promoted by the Monnaie de Paris (Paris Mint) in celebration of the signing of the European Act (one of 12 designers from the European Community invited to partake in the event). The design event is part of a programme launched to promote the art of the poster; the theme for poster, medal and first day cover was "Europe as a Communication and Cultural Field".

Posters for the Digital Design Bursary. A national student design bursary aimed at promoting design standards and awareness throughout Irish design colleges. Client: Digital Equipment Corporation bv

Posters

Submission for "Kiel Week", an annual international sailing event in Germany
Client: Kieler Woche Committee

Digital learning centre – based on typographic interplay of a series of quotations from Irish and English writers
Client: Digital Equipment Corporation bv

Exhibition on six city based artists' showing in the country
Client: Kilkenny Art Gallery Society

Kieler Woche 1981   20.-28. Juni

MERVUE LEARNING CENTRE

Exact
FULL
READY

Writing maketh an exact man

Reading maketh a full man

Conference maketh a ready man

SIX

Six
in the sticks

Dorothy Cross
Ned McLoughlin
Paula Minchin
Francis Tansey
Sam Walsh
Tony Sheehan

Performance by Tony
Sheehan Thursday
1st October at 8.00pm

Admission free
Grant aided by The Arts
Council/An Chomhairle
Ealaíon

Butler Gallery Kilkenny Castle   7 Nov-7 Dec. 10·30am-5pm. Tue-Sat

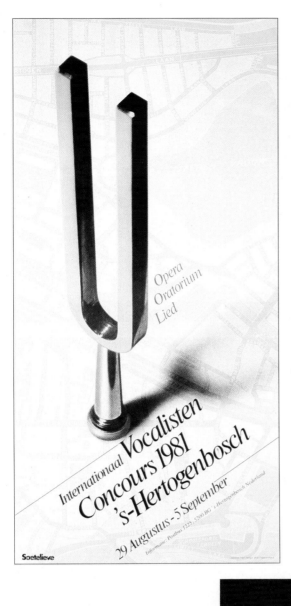

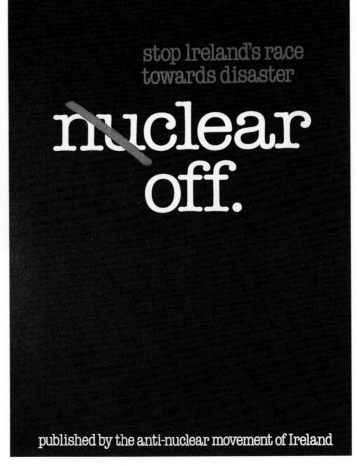

Posters

*Vocalisten Concours –
classical musical festival*
Client: Total Design
Amsterdam

Japanese Kno
Client: Kilkenny Arts
Week

Nuclear off
Client: Anti-nuclear
Movement of Ireland

Direction Out - art catalogue
Client: Douglas Hyde Gallery

Jacenta Feeney - art catalogue
Client: Arts Council of Ireland

Exhibition catalogue and poster
Client: Arts Council of Ireland

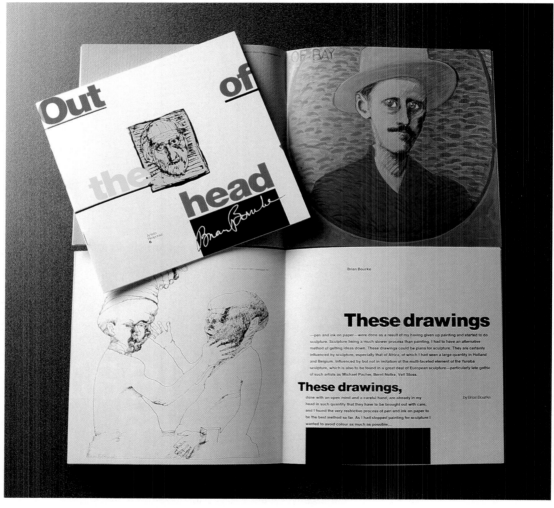

Poster and promotional material for Kilkenny Arts Week
Client: Kilkenny Arts Week

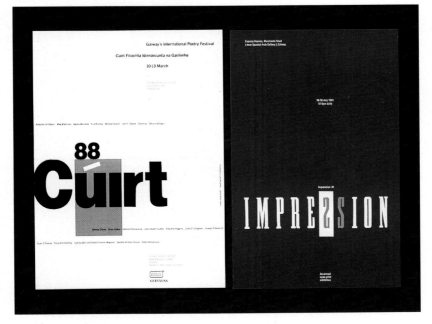

Cuirt 88 - Poster for poetry festival
Client: Arts Centre, Galway

Impression IV - annual printmakers exhibition
Client: Spanish Arch Gallery, Galway

*Promotional catalogues
of European software
products produced in six
languages
Client: Digital
Equipment
International bv*

Safety Handbook
Client: Digital
Equipment
International bv

Engineering review
board - promotional
booklet and forms for
self-paced learning
programme
Client: Digital
Equipment
International bv

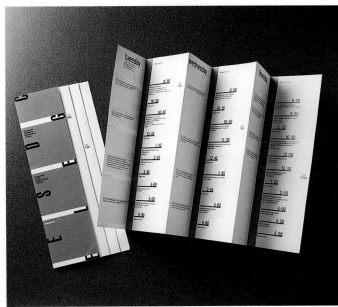

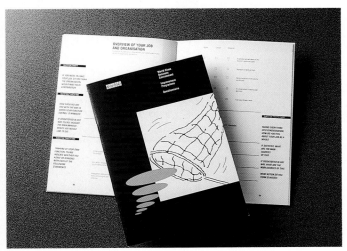

Three day conference
programme
Client: Digital
Equipment
International bv

Questionnaire booklet
based on sensing
employee attitudes
Client: Digital
Equipment
International bv

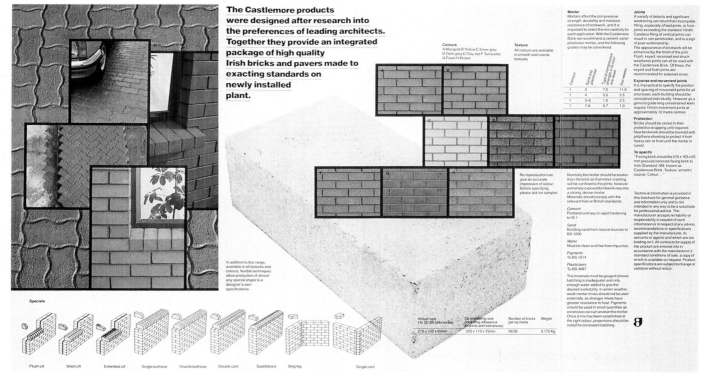

The Castlemore products were designed after research into the preferences of leading architects. Together they provide an integrated package of high quality Irish bricks and pavers made to exacting standards on newly installed plant.

In addition to this range, available in all textures and colours, flexible techniques allow production of almost any special shape to a designer's own specifications.

Colours
A Marigold B Yellow C Silver grey D Dark grey E Clay red F Terracotta G Fawn H Brown

Texture
All colours are available in both smooth and coarse textures

No reproduction can give an accurate impression of colour. Before specifying, please ask for samples.

Mortar
Mortars affect the compressive strength, durability and moisture resistance of brickwork, and it is important to select the mix carefully for each application. With the Castlemore Brick we recommend a cement-sand-plasticiser mortar, and the following grades may be considered.

Cement	Sand and plasticiser	Typical compressive strength in N/mm²	
		four weeks	
1	3	7.0	11.0
1	4	3.5	5.5
1	5-6	1.0	2.5
1	7-8	0.7	1.0

Normally the mortar should be weaker than the brick so that minor cracking will be confined to the joints; however extremely exposed brickwork requires a strong, dense mortar. Materials should comply with the relevant Irish or British standards:

Cement
Portland ordinary or rapid hardening to IS 1

Sand
Building sand from natural sources to BS 1200

Water
Must be clean and free from impurities

Pigments
To BS 1014

Plasticisers
To BS 4887

The materials must be gauged (shovel batching is inadequate) and only enough water added to give the desired workability. In winter weather, weak mortar mixes should not be used externally, as stronger mixes have greater resistance to frost. Pigments should be used in small quantities as excessive use can weaken the mortar. Once a mix has been established at the right colour, proportions should be noted for consistent batching.

Joints
A variety of defects and significant weakening can result from incomplete filling, especially of bed joints, or from joints exceeding the standard 10mm. Careless filling of vertical joints can result in rain penetration, and is a sign of poor workmanship.
The appearance of brickwork will be enhanced by the finish of the joint. Flush, keyed, recessed and struck weathered joints can all be used with the Castlemore Brick. Of these, the keyed and flush joints are recommended for exposed areas.

Expansion and movement joints
It is impractical to specify the position and spacing of movement joints for all structures; each building should be considered individually. However as a general guide long unrestrained walls require 10 mm movement joints at approximately 12 metre centres.

Protection
Bricks should be stored in their protective wrapping until required. New brickwork should be covered with polythene sheeting to protect it from heavy rain or frost until the mortar is cured.

To specify
"Facing brick should be 215 x 103 x 65 mm pressed concrete facing brick to Irish Standard 189, known as Castlemore Brick. Texture: smooth/coarse. Colour:..."

Technical information is provided in this brochure for general guidance and information only and is not intended in any way to be a substitute for professional advice. The manufacturer accepts no liability or responsibility in respect of such information or in respect of any advice, recommendations or specifications supplied by the manufacturer, its servants or agents and which are not binding on it. All contracts for supply of the product are entered into in accordance with the manufacturer's standard conditions of sale, a copy of which is available on request. Product specifications are subject to change or variation without notice.

Specials

Flush cill · Short cill · Extended cill · Single bullnose · Double bullnose · Double cant · Saddleback · Dog leg · Single cant

Actual size (to IS 189 tolerances)	Co-ordinating size (including allowance for joints and tolerances)	Number of bricks per sq metre	Weight
215 x 103 x 65mm	225 x 113 x 75mm	59.26	3.175 Kg

Leaflets for pave and brick manufacturer
Client: Castlemore Quarries

Part of a programme of redesign of forms for the Post Office
Client: Irish Post Office

Jerpoint Glass – identity for Kilkenny glassblower
Client: Keith Leadbetter

Catalogue of Contract Interiors
Client: Kilkenny Design Workshops

Design of symbol based on a stylised fingerprint, later applied to postage stamp by the German post office.
Client: European Patent Organisation

Catalogue of Contract Interiors
Client: Kilkenny Design Workshops

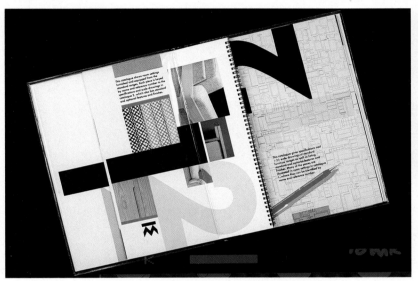

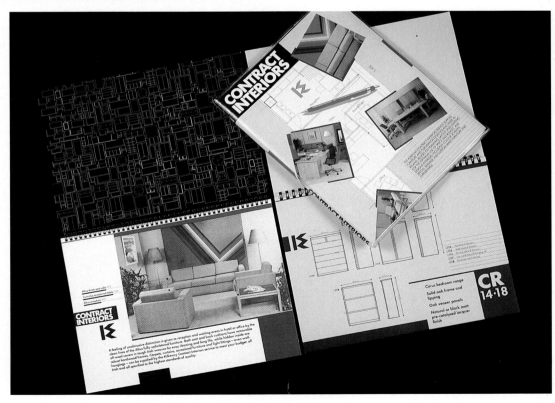

DENMARK

UNITED KINGDOM

GERMANY

IRELAND

LUXEMBOURG

NETHERLANDS

GREECE

BELGIUM

ITALY

FRANCE

SPAIN

PORTUGAL

Josep Pla-Narbona

Barcelona's beloved Josep Pla-Narbona was born in 1928. As a young man in 1945 he studied art at the Barcelona Art and Craft School until 1949, then spent two years on a professional sojourn in Paris. He returned to Barcelona in 1958 to set up his own studio and by 1961 had been twice awarded the Saint George prize for drawing, appointed professor of Advertising Plastic Art at the Massana School, and elected First Chairman of the 'Grafistas Agrupación FAD' which is known today as 'ADG-FAD'. In 1962, Pla-Narbona studied typographic techniques in Switzerland and worked with the advertising agency Adolf Wirz of Zurich, and produced a series of lithographies for the Zurich company ARTA. Since that time what has followed for Pla-Narbona has been yearly honours of exhibits, awards, and entrustments in his art and in his design work.

Pla-Narbona's design work has been exhibited throughout the world including the 1st International Biennale Poster exhibition in Warsaw, at the inauguration of the Lincoln Center, and the American Institute of Graphic Arts in New York. Pla-Narbona designed posters for both the 25th Olympic Games and the Spanish pavilion for the Universal Exhibition of Sevilla EXPO '92. The bibliographies on Pla-Narbona are many, and include E. Rabat's "The World Masters: 10 Josep Pla-Narbona", in 'IDEA' and M. Muller's "The Haunted World of José Pla-Narbona", 'Upper & Lower Case'. Pla-Narbona is currently chairman for Spain of the Alliance Graphique Internationale.

Josep Pla-Narbona's artistic and graphic work are recorded in the historical process experienced by Spain. He was a child of the Republic and the war, an adolescent and young man who learned his profession and formed his strong spirit in the crude postwar era and during the brutal dictatorship of the Franco regime. He was one of the professionals in the graphic arts and publicity who participated in the renewal movement of the early sixties. He channelled his work toward a new culture and a new concept of design which at the time in Spain, had no defined position.

Many of his posters from the fifties and sixties still live in the collective memory of the people, who recall the one which recommended an analgesic which would free you from a pain that hammered at your head with a gigantic fist, or the antidepressant which would put white wings on a darkened face, or figures with abstract faces shattered by the havoc of a flu epidemic. From the early days continuing on into the present day, all of his work has been conceived from an extraordinarily personal viewpoint. So much so that when one mentions a poster that he has created, it is talked about as a "Pla-Narbona."

From the beginning of his career, Pla-Narbona has not established clear differences between his artistic and design activities. He says, "I produce a Pla-Narbona at any time and according to the requirements of any commission. I do not establish any difference between my work as a designer and my work as a painter. In painting and graphic design the initial planning is the same."His work, whether it is an advertisement, a poster, a logo, a book design, or a painting, is always a challenge to communication. They are at play in free and intelligent associations, which are in the process of revealing an idea and delivering a message. The message finally reveals itself as something so direct yet diaphanous it has been described as having, "a loquacious brutality," and being "an intellectual game of interlocution."

Influenced by the doctrines of Sigmund Freud, by the artistic experiences of surrealism, and above all stamped by a vision of the world so corrosive, imaginative, and personal, Pla-Narbona, through his pictorial and design work, has created his own language that melds the brutally real with the dreamlike and poetic. His reality stands independent of the work, and always carries the unmistakable seal of a "Pla-Narbona."

Poster

*Barcelona '92 Olympic
Games
Client: COOB '92, S.A.*

Sección Española para la Exposición Universal de Sevilla, 1992

Posters

*Sección Española para
la Exposición Universal
de Sevilla*

*Promoting visit to the
Zoologicial Park of
Barcelona
Client: Municipal
Council of Barcelona*

*Exhibition of paintings
Client: Altarriba Art, S.A.*

AMERICA'S GRAPHIC DESIGN MAGAZINE
MARCH/APRIL 1970
PRINT XXIV:II **Print**

Pla Narbona

Cover

Print Magazine
Client: Martin Fox
(publisher)

Cefaleas debidas
a cambios meteorológicos

Cefaleas de origen
digestivo y ginecológico

Cefaleas por abuso
de alcohol y tabaco

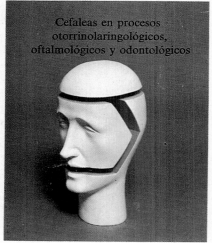

Cefaleas en procesos
otorrinolaringológicos,
oftalmológicos y odontológicos

Cefaleas causadas
por el «stress» ciudadano

Cefaleas de los lábiles tensionales

*Advertisements for
pharmaceutical product
to treat headache
Client: Sandoz S.A.*

Nuevo **Tonopán** Sandoz

en las cefaleas causadas por el «stress» ciudadano

si el zapato hablara, diría...

si el pie y el zapato hablaran, dirían...

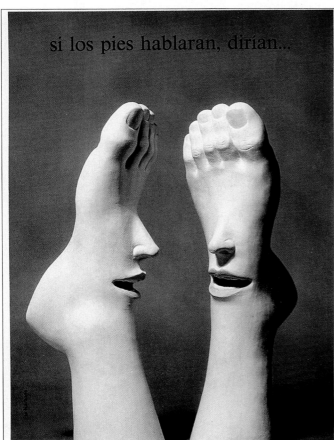

si los pies hablaran, dirían...

Advertisements for
JO.RI.GU socks
Client: José Riera Gubau
S.A.

Book covers

Caleidoscopio 4 gráficos
Client: Editorial Blume,
S.A.

*Readings of Jacint
Verdaguer*
Client: Ediciones
Destino, S.A.

*Readings of Joan
Maragall*
Client: Ediciones
Destino, S.A.

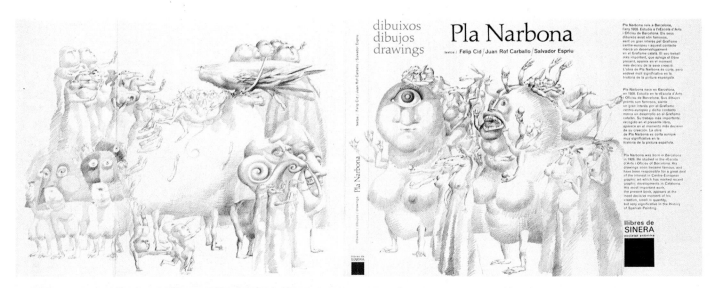

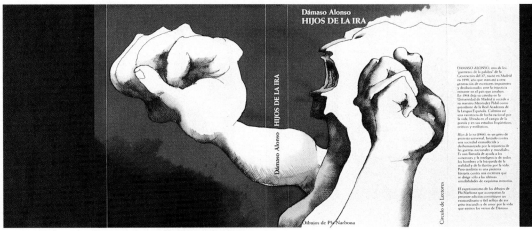

Book covers

Pla Narbona Drawings
Client: Llibres de Sinera,
S.A.

Hijos de la Ira of
Dámaso Alonso
Client: Circulo de
Lectores, S.A.

Poetry of Pedro Salinas
Client: Circulo de
Lectores, S.A.

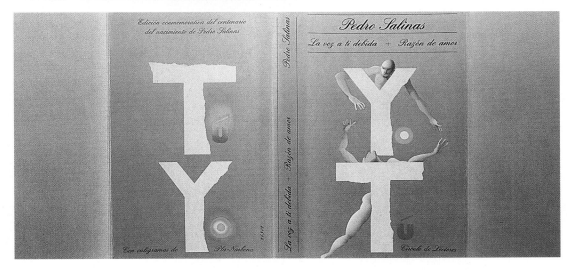

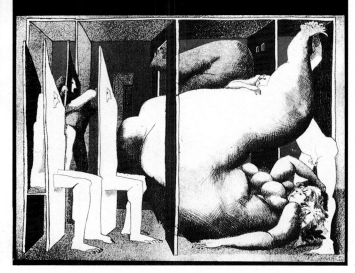

Book covers

*San Camilo, 1936 of
Camilo José Cela
Client: Editorial Noguer,
S.A.*

*Oficio de tinieblas of
Camilo José Cela
Client: Editorial Noguer,
S.A.*

*San Camilo, 1936 of
Camilo José Cela
Client: Ediciones
Alfaguara, S.A.*

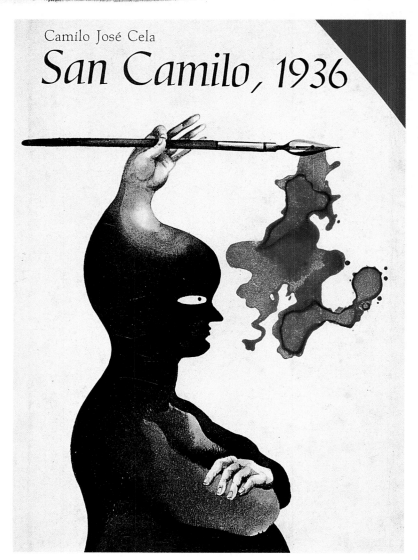

Revista de la *Alta Fidelidad*

Diciembre, 1971 — 50 Ptas.

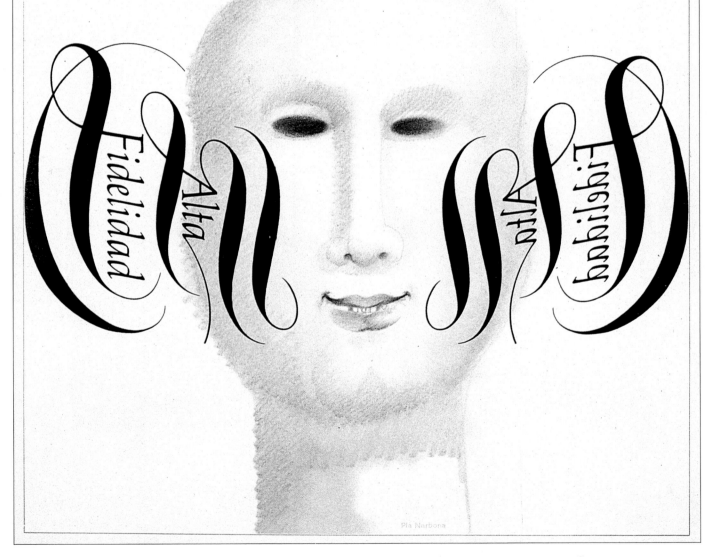

El renacimiento de Gustav Mahler. Bolsa del aficionado. Jazz actualidad. Rememoranza Navideña. Mirilla discográfica. Entrevista con el Presidente de Juventudes Musicales.

Pla Narbona

Cover

*Alta fidelidad magazine
Client: Editorial Pro-música (Barcelona)*

Varices del embarazo **Venoruton**®

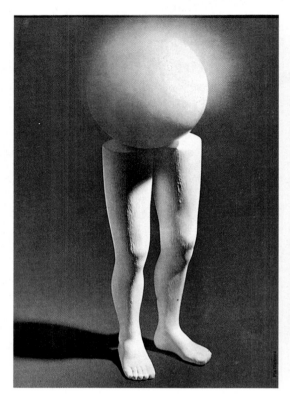

Piernas pesadas **Venoruton**®

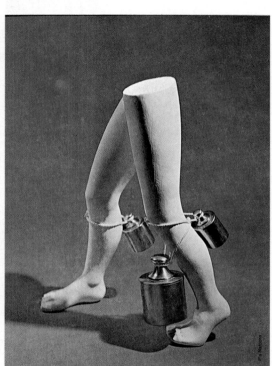

pintura de Pla Narbona

Equilibrio, control y seguridad durante 24 horas

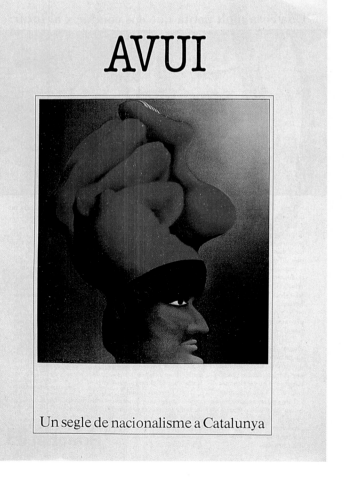

AVUI

Un segle de nacionalisme a Catalunya

3ᴬ BIENAL INTERNACIONAL DE ARTES APLICADAS PUNTA DEL ESTE URUGUAY

Pla-Narbona

Poster for 3ª Bienal
Internacional de Artes
Aplicadas. Punta del
Este, Uruguay

Client: Delegation of the
Spanish Government to
South America

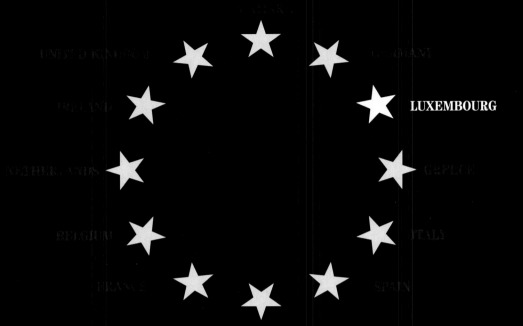

DENMARK

UNITED KINGDOM

GERMANY

IRELAND

LUXEMBOURG

NETHERLANDS

GREECE

BELGIUM

ITALY

FRANCE

SPAIN

PORTUGAL

Kamen Popov

Kamen Popov was born in Sofia, Bulgaria in 1947. In 1973 he graduated in Applied Graphics at the Arts Academy. He was Art Director at 'Septemvri' Publishers in Sofia from 1979 to 1987, and since 1988 he has been Art Director for Biensfeld Editions in Luxembourg. Many articles on the work and life of Kamen Popov have appeared in publications throughout the world including: PPC International, New York; Media, Paris; and Idea, Tokyo.

Popov has participated in and received numerous Diplomas and Certificates of honour from the Biennals of Warsaw, Lahti, Mons, Art Directors Club, and ZGRAF. He also received prizes from the Brno Biennals of 1986 and 1990. The works of Popov are honoured internationally in the museums of Munich, Essen, New York, Jerusalem, Paris, and Luxembourg. Almost every year since 1981 Popov has had personal showings in the renown art galleries of Luxembourg, Belgium, France, the U.S., and Germany.

I prefer a simple, almost laconic style. Every superfluous element which could weigh down a poster must be left out. In the course of my work, perhaps the most difficult task is discovering what I can leave out. It is only after the successive 'cleaning up' of a graphic work of everything that is insignificant that one achieves a strong, impressive and simple style. I like to live with the rhythm of our time and to feel like a citizen of our planet, and I have chosen the area of graphic poster because I love to be laconic. The fact that I have no preference for precisely given themes allows me a wide range of poster graphic applications. Whether social or cultural, or publicity posters, their themes all give me the opportunity to react to the events of our time.

The idea for a poster comes mostly when I am walking in the street observing the people. I can link their reactions to an event, and later the idea comes to paper in a graphic form. The theme of my posters determines the graphic means I use to realise them - one time it will be a drawing, and yet at other times it can be a photograph, or other graphic combinations. When creating a poster I keep in mind that it must be accessible to everyone and must be immediately understood by the greatest number possible. The poster is a way of direct and quick communication, and if it achieves that then mostly it is a 'good' poster.

But essential for a poster is its idea. It mustn't be 'talking' a lot of detail. It must be one cry. Weak crying will not always be heard by everyone but if it is one strong, single cry then everyone will hear and understand. My final aim and probably greatest difficulty is to find this one idea and express it in one cry. The logo I use comes from a poster I designed to participate in at the 1976 Warsaw Biennale. The theme of the exhibition was "Habitat." This black & white poster won an award and, I think, reflects most of my concepts and ideas of what a poster should be: brief, clear, understood by as many as possible, and a single 'cry' of which the image remains in people's minds.

Poster

*Exhibition of Posters by
Kamen Popov in
Strasbourg, France
sponsored by the Bank
CIAL, France*

JACQUES ET SON MAITRE
MILAN KUNDERA
Avec: Valérie Bodson
Patricia Fichant
Brigitte Krüger
Claudine Pelletier
Jean-Paul Bissieux
Louis Bonnet
Claude Frisoni
Alain-Jean Miche
Marc Olinger
Jacques Paquer
Charles Suberville
mise en scène: Maurice Travail
assistante: Renée Maerz
décor et costumes: Jeanny Kratochwil
24 octobre abo F2
+ vente libre, 20.30 heures
25 octobre 20.30 heures
10 novembre abo E2b
+ vente libre, 20.30 heures
22 novembre abo E2j
+ vente libre, 18.30 heures
23 novembre abo E2a
20.30 heures
26 novembre abo E2k
+ vente libre, 18.30 heures
29 novembre 18.30 heures
théâtre des capucins
Réservations: Caisse du théâtre entre 16 et 19 heures, téléphone: 22 06 45 entre 14 et 19 heures
KAMEN POPOV

Poster

Theatre play "The Miser by Moliere", Theatre of Capucins, Luxembourg

Poster

*Theatre play "George
Dandin or the
Dumbfounded
Husband", Theatre of
Capucins, Luxembourg*

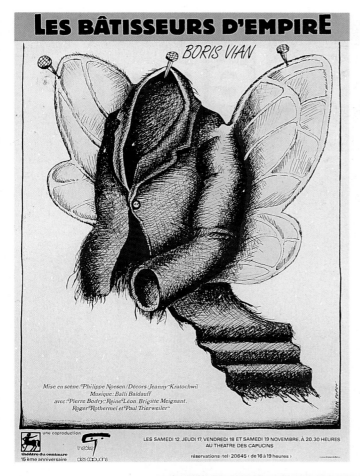

Posters

Theatre play "Builders of an Empire" by Boris Vian, Theatre de Saintore, Luxembourg

Theatre play "The Barber of Seville" by Beaumarchais, Theatre des Capucins, Luexmbourg

Theatre play "Waiting for Godot" by Samuel Becket, Theatre des Capucins, Luxembourg

Poster

Theatre play "Closed
Outside" by Claude
Frisoni, The Small
Theatre of Luxembourg

Poster

Theatre play "Exercise of Styles" by Raymond Queneau, Theatre de Saintore, Luxembourg

Posters

"Don't Run a Risk at your Work-Place" –Du Pont, Security Department, Luxembourg

Save Africa – a concert organised by the Town Hall in Luxembourg

Green Light for the ECU, The Department of Luxembourg in the European Community

200 Years French Revolution "Liberty, Equality, Fraternity" for the French Cultural Centre in Luxembourg

KAMEN·POPOV
AFFICHES

POSTERS
Grace Gallery, 11th fl. Namm Hall **New York City Technical College**
NOVEMBER 2-18, 1988
300 Jay Street, Brooklyn. Gallery open Monday - Friday 10:00 AM - 4:00 PM (718) 643-8378(9)

Posters

*Exhibition of Posters by
Kamen Popov, Grace
Gallery of the New York
City Technical College*

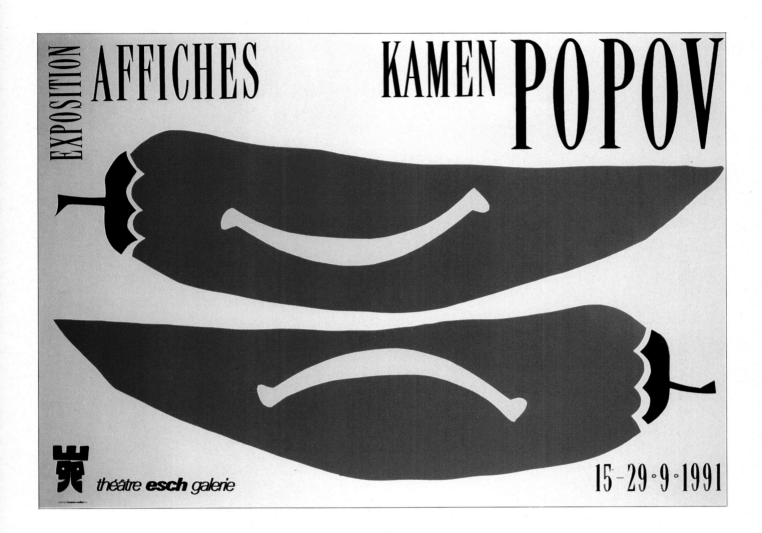

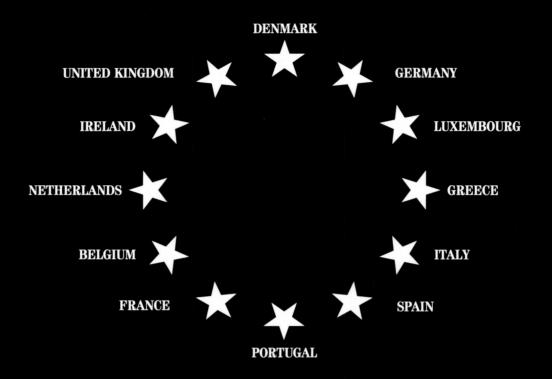

Per Arnodi

Toldbodgade 77
DK-1253 Copenhagen
Denmark
Tel: + 45 33 14008
Fax: +45 33 140184

Pierre Bernard

*Atelier de Création
Graphique*
33 Rue du Faubourg
Poissonnière
75009 Paris
France
Tel: +33 (1) 48 01 95 95
Fax: +33 (1) 48 01 95 96

Pieter Brattinga

*Form Mediation
International*
Prinsengracht 628
1017 KT Amsterdam
Netherlands
Tel: +31 (20) 6 22 42 65
Fax: +31 (20) 6 26 74 60

Antero Ferreira

Antero Ferreira Design
Rua de Roriz 203
4100 Porto
Portugal
Tel: +351 (2) 6104657
Fax: +351 (2) 6104757

Gilles Fiszman

*Axion Fiszman +
Partners, sprl*
Avenue Emile Duray 18
B-1050 Bruxelles
Belgium
Tel: +32 (2) 647 21 20
Fax: +32 (2) 640 66 48

Alan Fletcher

Pentagram Design
11 Needham Road
London W11 2RP
England
Tel: +44 (71) 229 3477
Fax: +44 (71) 727 9932

Michael Katzourakis

A + M Katzourakis
7, Zalokosta Street
106 71 Athens
Greece
Tel: +30 (1) 3608247,
3613767
Fax: +30 (1) 3611109

Italo Lupi

39 Via Vigevano
20144 Milano
Italy
Tel: +39 (2) 89 40 39 50
Fax: +39 (2) 89 40 40 42

Pierre Mendell

Mendell & Oberer
Widenmayerstrasse 12
8000 München 22
Germany
Tel: +49 (89) 224055
Fax: +49 (89) 2913505

Tony O'Hanlon

Leitriff House
Letteragh
Galway, Ireland
Tel/Fax: +353 (91)
22786

Pla-Narbona

Pla-Narbona
c/ Papallones 4
08190 Sant Cugat del
Vallès
Barcelona
Spain
Tel: +34 (93) 675.52.95

Kamen Popov

Gallery Edition 88
4, Rue Louvigny
L-1946 Luxembourg
Tel: +352 474599
Fax: +352 474597